PICNIC

"The summer's flower is to the summer sweet,
Though to itself it only live and die."
SHAKESPEARE—Sonnet 94

 RANDOM HOUSE · NEW YORK

PICNIC

A Summer Romance in Three Acts

by WILLIAM INGE

COPYRIGHT, 1953, BY WILLIAM INGE

Photographs by Zinn Arthur

TO
JOSH LOGAN

Who gave of himself unsparingly in helping me to realize the play. I shall be always grateful.

Picnic was produced by The Theatre Guild and Joshua Logan, at the Music Box Theatre, New York City on February 19, 1953, with the following cast:

HELEN POTTS	*Ruth McDevitt*
HAL CARTER	*Ralph Meeker*
MILLIE OWENS	*Kim Stanley*
BOMBER	*Morris Miller*
MADGE OWENS	*Janice Rule*
FLO OWENS	*Peggy Concklin*
ROSEMARY SYDNEY	*Eileen Heckart*
ALAN SEYMOUR	*Paul Newman*
IRMA KRONKITE	*Reta Shaw*
CHRISTINE SCHOENWALDER	*Elizabeth Wilson*
HOWARD BEVANS	*Arthur O'Connell*

Directed by Joshua Logan

Scenery and Lighting by Jo Mielziner

SCENE

The action of the play takes place in a small Kansas town in the yard shared by Flo Owens and Helen Potts.

ACT ONE

Early morning, Labor Day.

ACT TWO

Late the same afternoon.

ACT THREE

Scene I.—Very early the following morning.
Scene II.—A few hours later.

ACT ONE

ACT ONE

The action of the play is laid on the porches and in the yards of two small houses that sit close beside each other in a small Kansas town. The house at the right belongs to MRS. FLORA OWENS, *a widow lady of about forty who lives there with her two young daughters,* MADGE *and* MILLIE. *The audience sees only a section of the house, from the doorstep and the front door extending to the back door, a porch lining all of the house that we see.*

The house at the left is inhabited by MRS. HELEN POTTS, *another but older widow lady who lives with her aged and invalid mother. Just the back of her house is visible, with steps leading up to the back door. Down farther is a woodshed, attached to the house by the roof. The space between woodshed and house forms a narrow passageway leading to the rest of* MRS. POTTS' *property. The yard between the houses is used interchangeably by members of both houses for visiting and relaxation.*

Both houses are humble dwellings built with no other pretension than to provide comfortable shelter for their occupants. The ladies cannot always afford to keep their houses painted, but they work hard to maintain a tidy appearance, keeping the yards clean, watching the flower beds, supplying colorful slip covers for the porch furniture.

Behind the houses is a stretch of picket fence with a gateway leading from the sidewalk into the yard between the houses. Beyond the fence, in the distance, is the panorama of a typical small Midwestern town, including a grain elevator,

3

a railway station, a great silo and a church steeple, all blessed from above by a high sky of innocent blue.

The curtain rises on an empty, sunlit stage. It is early morning in late summer, Labor Day, and autumn has just begun to edge the green landscape with a rim of brown. Dew is still on the landscape and mist rises from the earth in the distance. MRS. POTTS *appears on her back porch, at left. She is a merry, dumpy little woman close to sixty. She comes down the steps and stands before the woodshed, waiting for* HAL CARTER *to follow.* HAL *comes out carrying a basket of trash on his shoulder, an exceedingly handsome, husky youth dressed in T-shirt, dungarees and cowboy boots. In a past era he would have been called a vagabond, but* HAL *today is usually referred to as a bum.* MRS. POTTS *speaks to him.*

MRS. POTTS

You just had a big breakfast. Wouldn't you like to rest a while before you go to work?

HAL
(*Managing to sound cheerful*)
Work's good for my digestion, Mam.

MRS. POTTS

Now, stop being embarrassed because you asked for breakfast.

HAL

I never did it before.

MRS. POTTS

What's the difference? We all have misfortune part of the time.

HAL

Seems to me, Mam, like I have it *lots* of the time.

(*Then they laugh together.* MRS. POTTS *leads him off
through the passageway. In a moment,* MILLIE OWENS
*bursts out of the kitchen door of the house, right. She
is a wiry kid of sixteen, boisterous and assertive, but
likable when one begins to understand that she is trying to disguise her basic shyness. Her secret habit is
to come outside after breakfast and enjoy her morning cigarette where her mother will not see her. She
is just lighting up when* BOMBER, *the newsboy, appears at the back gate and slings a paper noisily
against the house. This gives* MILLIE *a chance to as-
sail him.*)

MILLIE

Hey, Crazy, wanta knock the house down?

BOMBER

(*A tough kid about* MILLIE's *age*)

I don't hear you.

MILLIE

If you ever break a window, you'll hear me.

BOMBER

Go back to bed.

MILLIE

Go blow your nose.

BOMBER

(*With a look at the upper window of the house
which presumably marks* MADGE's *room*)

Go back to bed and tell your pretty sister to come out. It's no fun lookin' at you. (MILLIE *ignores him.* BOMBER *doesn't intend to let her*) I'm talkin' to *you*, Goonface!

MILLIE
(*Jumping to her feet and tearing into* BOMBER *with flying fists*)
You take that back, you ornery bastard. You take that back.

BOMBER
(*Laughing, easily warding off her blows*)
Listen to Goonface! She cusses just like a man.

MILLIE
(*Goes after him with doubled fists*)
I'll kill you, you ornery bastard! I'll *kill* you!

BOMBER
(*Dodging her fists*)
Lookit Mrs. Tar-zan! Lookit Mrs. Tar-zan!

MADGE
(MADGE *comes out of the back door. She is an un-usually beautiful girl of eighteen, who seems to take her beauty very much for granted. She wears sandals and a simple wash dress. She has just shampooed her hair and is now scrubbing her head with a towel*)
Who's making so much noise?

BOMBER
(*With a shy grin*)
Hi, Madge!

MADGE

Hi, Bomber.

BOMBER

I hope I didn't wake you, Madge, or bother you or anything.

MADGE

Nothing bothers me.

BOMBER

(*Warming up*)

Hey, Madge, a bunch of us guys are chippin' in on a hotrod—radio and everything. I get it every Friday night.

MADGE

I'm not one of those girls that jump in a hot-rod every time you boys turn a corner and honk. If a boy wants a date with me, he can come to the door like a gentleman and ask if I'm in.

MILLIE

Alan Seymour sends her flowers every time they go out.

BOMBER

(*To* MADGE)

I can't send you flowers, Baby—but I can *send* you!

MILLIE

Listen to him braggin'.

BOMBER

(*Persisting*)

Lemme pick you up some night after Seymour brings you home.

MADGE
(*A trifle haughty*)
That wouldn't be fair to Alan. We go steady.

MILLIE
Don't you know what "steady" means, stupid?

BOMBER
I seen you riding around in his Cadillac like you was a duchess. Why do good-looking girls have to be so stuck on themselves?

MADGE
(*Jumps up, furious*)
I'm not stuck on myself! You take that back, Bomber Gutzel!

BOMBER
(*Still persisting*)
Lemme pick you up some night! Please! (MADGE *walks away to evade him but* BOMBER *is close behind her*) We'll get some cans of beer and go down to the river road and listen to music on the radio.

(HAL CARTER *has come on from right and put a rake in the woodshed. He observes the scene between* MADGE *and* BOMBER.)

MILLIE
(*Laughing at* BOMBER)
Wouldn't that be romantic!

BOMBER
(*Grabbing* MADGE's *arm*)
C'mon, Madge, give a guy a break!

HAL
(*To* BOMBER)

On your way, lover boy!

BOMBER
(*Turning*)

Who're *you*?

HAL

What's that matter? I'm bigger'n you are.
(BOMBER *looks at* HAL, *feels a little inadequate, and starts off.*)

MILLIE
(*Calling after* BOMBER)

Go peddle your papers!

(*Gives* BOMBER *a raspberry as he disappears with papers.*)

HAL
(*To* MILLIE)

Got a smoke, kid? (MILLIE *gives* HAL *a cigarette, wondering who he is*) Thanks, kid.

MILLIE

You workin' for Mrs. Potts?

HAL

Doin' a few jobs in the yard.

MILLIE

She give you breakfast?

HAL
(*Embarrassed about it*)

Yah.

MADGE

Millie! Mind your business.

HAL
(Turning to MADGE, *his face lighting)*

Hi.

MADGE

Hi.

*(*MADGE *and* HAL *stand looking at each other, awkward and self-conscious.* FLO, *the mother, comes out almost immediately, as though she had sensed* HAL's *presence.* FLO *carries a sewing basket in one arm and a party dress over the other. She is a rather impatient little woman who has worked hard for ten years or more to serve as both father and mother to her girls. One must feel that underneath a certain hardness in her character there is a deep love and concern for the girls. She regards* HAL *suspiciously.)*

FLO

Young man, this is *my* house. Is there something you want?

HAL

Just loafin', Mam.

FLO

This is a busy day for us. We have no time to loaf.

(There is a quick glance between HAL *and* FLO, *as though each sized up the other as a potential threat.)*

HAL

You the mother?

FLO

Yes. You better run along now.

HAL

Like you say, Lady. It's your house.
(*With a shrug of the shoulders, he saunters off stage.*)

FLO

Has Helen Potts taken in another tramp?

MADGE

I don't see why he's a tramp just because Mrs. Potts gave
him breakfast.

FLO

I'm going to speak to her about the way she takes in every
Tom, Dick and Harry!

MADGE

He wasn't doing any harm.

FLO

I bet he'd like to. (*Sits on the porch and begins sewing on
party dress. To* MADGE) Have you called Alan this morning?

MADGE

I haven't had time.

MILLIE

He's coming by pretty soon to take us swimming.

FLO
(*To* MADGE)

Tell him they're expecting a big crowd at the park this
evening, so he'd better use his father's influence at the City
Hall to reserve a table. Oh, and tell him to get one down by
the river, close to a Dutch oven.

MADGE

He'll think I'm being bossy.

FLO

Alan is the kind of man who doesn't mind if a woman's bossy.
(*A train whistle in the distance.* MADGE *listens.*)

MADGE

Whenever I hear that train coming to town, I always get a little feeling of excitement—in here.
(*Hugging her stomach.*)

MILLIE

Whenever I hear it, I tell myself I'm going to get on it some day and go to New York.

FLO

That train just goes as far as Tulsa.

MILLIE

In Tulsa I could catch another train.

MADGE

I always wonder, maybe some wonderful person is getting off here, just by accident, and he'll come into the dime store for something and see me behind the counter, and he'll study me very strangely and then decide I'm just the person they're looking for in Washington for an important job in the Espionage Department. (*She is carried away*) Or maybe he wants me for some great medical experiment that'll save the whole human race.

FLO

Things like that don't happen in dime stores. (*Changing the subject*) Millie, would you take the milk inside?

MILLIE
(*As she exits into kitchen with milk*)
Awwww.

FLO
(*After a moment*)
Did you and Alan have a good time on your date last night?

MADGE

Uh-huh.

FLO

What'd you do?

MADGE

We went over to his house and he played some of his classical records.

FLO
(*After a pause*)
Then what'd you do?

MADGE

Drove over to Cherryvale and had some barbecue.

FLO
(*A hard question to ask*)
Madge, does Alan ever—make love?

MADGE

When we drive over to Cherryvale we always park the car by the river and get real romantic.

FLO

Do you let him kiss you? After all, you've been going together all summer.

MADGE

Of course I let him.

FLO

Does he ever want to go beyond kissing?

MADGE
(*Embarrassed*)

Mom!

FLO

I'm your mother, for heaven's sake! These things have to be talked about. Does he?

MADGE

Well—yes.

FLO

Does Alan get mad if you—won't?

MADGE

No.

FLO
(*To herself, puzzled*)

He doesn't . . .

MADGE

Alan's not like *most* boys. He doesn't wanta do anything he'd be sorry for.

FLO

Do *you* like it when he kisses you?

MADGE

Yes.

FLO

You don't sound very enthusiastic.

MADGE

What do you expect me to do—pass out every time Alan puts his arm around me?

FLO

No, you don't have to pass out. (*Gives* MADGE *the dress she has been sewing on*) Here. Hold this dress up in front of you. (*She continues*) It'd be awfully nice to be married to Alan. You'd live in comfort the rest of your life, with charge accounts at all the stores, automobiles and trips. You'd be invited by all his friends to parties in their homes and at the Country Club.

MADGE

(*A confession*)

Mom, I don't feel right with those people.

FLO

Why not? You're as good as they are.

MADGE

I know, Mom, but all of Alan's friends talk about college and trips to Europe. I feel left out.

FLO

You'll get over those feelings in time. Alan will be going back to school in a few weeks. You better get busy.

MADGE

Busy what?

FLO

A pretty girl doesn't have long—just a few years. Then she's the equal of kings and she can walk out of a shanty like this and live in a palace with a doting husband who'll spend his life making her happy.

MADGE
(*To herself*)

I know.

FLO

Because once, *once* she was young and pretty. If she loses her chance then, she might as well throw all her prettiness away.
(*Giving* MADGE *the dress.*)

MADGE
(*Holding the dress before her as* FLO *checks length*)

I'm only eighteen.

FLO

And next summer you'll be nineteen, and then twenty, and then twenty-one, and then the years'll start going by so fast you'll lose count of them. First thing you know, you'll be forty, still selling candy at the dime store.

MADGE

You don't have to get morbid.

MILLIE
(*Comes out with sketch book, sees* MADGE *holding dress before her*)

Everyone around here gets to dress up and go places except me.

MADGE

Alan said he'd try to find you a date for the picnic tonight.

MILLIE

I don't want Alan asking any of these crazy boys in town to take me anywhere.

MADGE

Beggars can't be choosers!

MILLIE

You shut up.

FLO

Madge, that was mean. There'll be dancing at the pavilion tonight. Millie should have a date, too.

MADGE

If she wants a date, why doesn't she dress up and act decent?

MILLIE

Cause I'm gonna dress and act the way I want to, and if you don't like it you know what you can do!

MADGE

Always complaining because she doesn't have any friends, but she smells so bad people don't want to be near her!

FLO

Girls, don't fight.

MILLIE
(*Ignoring* FLO)
La-de-da! Madge is the pretty one—but she's so dumb they
almost had to burn the schoolhouse down to get *her* out of it!
(*She mimics* MADGE.)

MADGE
That's not so!

MILLIE
Oh, isn't it? You never would have graduated if it hadn't
been for Jumpin' Jeeter.

FLO
(*Trying at least to keep up with the scrap*)
Who's Jumpin' Jeeter?

MILLIE
Teaches history. Kids call him Jumpin' Jeeter cause he's
so *jumpy* with all the pretty girls in his classes. He was flunk-
ing Madge till she went in his room and cried, and said . . .
(*Resorting again to mimicry*) "I just don't know what I'll do
if I don't pass history!"

MADGE
Mom, she's making that up.

MILLIE
Like fun I am! You couldn't even pass Miss Sydney's course
in shorthand and you have to work in the dime store!

MADGE
(*The girls know each other's most sensitive spots*)
You *are* a goon!

FLO
(*Giving up*)

Oh, girls!

MILLIE
(*Furious*)

Madge, you slut! You take that back or I'll kill you!

> (*She goes after* MADGE, *who screams and runs on the porch.*)

FLO

Girls! What will the neighbors say!

> (MILLIE *gets hold of* MADGE's *hair and yanks.* FLO *has to intercede.*)

MILLIE

No one can call me goon and get by with it!

FLO

You called her worse names!

MILLIE

It doesn't hurt what names I call her! She's pretty, so names don't bother her at all! She's pretty, so nothing else matters.

> (*She storms inside.*)

FLO

Poor Millie!

MADGE
(*Raging at the injustice*)

All I ever hear is "poor Millie," and poor Millie won herself a scholarship for four whole years of college!

FLO

A girl like Millie can need confidence in other ways.

(*This quiets* MADGE. *There is a silence.*)

MADGE
(*Subdued*)

Mom, do you love Millie more than me?

FLO

Of course not!

MADGE

Sometimes you act like you did.

FLO
(*With warmth, trying to effect an understanding*)

You were the first born. Your father thought the sun rose and set in you. He used to carry you on his shoulder for all the neighborhood to see. But things were different when Millie came.

MADGE

How?

FLO
(*With misgivings*)

They were just—different. Your father wasn't home much. The night Millie was born he was with a bunch of his wild friends at the road house.

MADGE

I loved Dad.

FLO
(*A little bitterly*)
Oh, everyone loved your father.

MADGE

Did you?

FLO
(*After a long pause of summing up*)
Some women are humiliated to love a man.

MADGE

Why?

FLO
(*Thinking as she speaks*)
Because—a woman is weak to begin with, I suppose, and
sometimes—her love for him makes her feel—almost help-
less. And maybe she fights him—'cause her love makes her
seem so dependent.

(*There is another pause.* MADGE *ruminates.*)

MADGE
Mom, what good is it to be pretty?

FLO

What a question!

MADGE

I mean it.

FLO
Well—pretty things are rare in this life.

MADGE

But what good are they?

FLO

Well—pretty things—like flowers and sunsets and rubies
—and pretty girls, too—they're like billboards telling us life
is good.

MADGE

But where do *I* come in?

FLO

What do you mean?

MADGE

Maybe I get tired being looked at.

FLO

Madge!

MADGE

Well, maybe I do!

FLO

Don't talk so selfish!

MADGE

I don't care if I *am* selfish. It's no good just being pretty.
It's no good!

HAL
(*Comes running on from passageway*)
Mam, is it all right if I start a fire?

FLO
(*Jumps to see* HAL)
What?

HAL
The nice lady, she said it's a hot enough day already and maybe you'd object.

FLO
(*Matter-of-factly*)
I guess we can stand it.

HAL
Thank you, Mam.

(HAL *runs off.*)

FLO
(*Looking after him*)
He just moves right in whether you want him to or not!

MADGE
I knew you wouldn't like him when I first saw him.

FLO
Do *you?*

MADGE
I don't like him or dislike him. I just wonder what he's like.

(ROSEMARY SYDNEY *makes a sudden, somewhat cavalier entrance out of the front door. She is a roomer, probably as old as* FLO *but would never admit it. Her hair is plastered to her head with wave-set and she wears a flowered kimono.*)

ROSEMARY

Anyone mind if an old-maid schoolteacher joins their company?

FLO

Sit down, Rosemary.

ROSEMARY

Mail come yet?

FLO

No mail today. It's Labor Day.

ROSEMARY

I forgot. I thought I might be gettin' a letter from that man I met at the high-school picnic last spring. (*A bawdy laugh*) Been wantin' to marry me ever since. A nice fellow and a peck of fun, but I don't have time for any of 'em when they start gettin' serious on me.

FLO

You schoolteachers are mighty independent!

(MILLIE *wanders out of kitchen, reading a book.*)

ROSEMARY

Shoot! I lived this long without a man. I don't see what's to keep me from getting *on* without one.

FLO

What about Howard?

ROSEMARY

Howard's just a friend-boy—not a boy friend. (MADGE *and* MILLIE *giggle at this.* ROSEMARY *sniffs the air*) I smell smoke.

FLO

Helen Potts is having her leaves burned. Smells kind of good, doesn't it?

ROSEMARY
(*Seeing* HAL *off stage*)

Who's the young man?

FLO

Just another no-good Helen Potts took in.

ROSEMARY
(*Very concerned*)

Mrs. Owens, he's working over there with his shirt off. I don't think that's right in the presence of ladies.

FLO
(*As* MILLIE *runs to look*)

Get away from there, Millie!

MILLIE
(*Returning to doorstep*)

Gee whiz! I go swimming every day and the boys don't have on half as much as he does now.

FLO

Swimming's different!

MILLIE

Madge, can I use your manicure set, just for kicks?

MADGE

If you promise not to get it messy.

(MILLIE *picks up the set and begins to experiment.*)

FLO
(*Looking off at* HAL)
Look at him showing off!

ROSEMARY
(*Turning away with propriety*)
Who does he think is interested?

(*She continues to massage her face.*)

FLO
(*To* ROSEMARY)
What's that you're rubbing in?

ROSEMARY
Ponsella Three-Way Tissue Cream. Makes a good base for your make-up.

FLO
There was an article in *The Reader's Digest* about some woman who got skin poisoning from using all those face creams.

ROSEMARY
Harriett Bristol—she's the American History teacher—she got ahold of some of that beauty clay last winter and it darn near took her skin off. All we girls thought she had leprosy!

(*She manages one more glance back at* HAL.)

MILLIE
(*Laboring over her manicure*)
Madge, how do you do your right hand?

MADGE
If you were nicer to people, maybe people would do something nice for *you* some time.

ROSEMARY

You got a beau, Millie?

MILLIE

No!

ROSEMARY

You can't kid me! Girls don't paint their fingernails unless they think some boy is gonna take notice.

FLO

Madge, will you try this dress on now, dear?

(MADGE *goes inside with the dress.*)

MRS. POTTS
(*Appears on her back porch, carrying a bundle of wet laundry*)

Flo!

FLO
(*Calling back, a noise like an owl*)

Hoooo!

MRS. POTTS

Are you going to be using the clothesline this morning?

FLO

I don't think so.

MRS. POTTS' MOTHER
(*An aged and quivering voice that still retains its command, issuing from the upper window of the house, left*)

Helen! Helen!

MRS. POTTS
(*Calling back*)
I'm hanging out the clothes, Mama. I'll be right back.

(*She goes busily off stage through the passageway.*)

FLO
(*Confidentially to* ROSEMARY)
Poor Helen! She told me sometimes she has to get up
three times a night to take her mother to the bathroom.

ROSEMARY
Why doesn't she put her in an old ladies' home?

FLO
None of 'em will take her. She's too mean.

ROSEMARY
She must be mean—if that story is true.

FLO
It *is* true! Helen and the Potts boy *ran off* and got married. Helen's mother caught her that very day and had the
marriage annulled!

ROSEMARY
(*With a shaking of her head*)
She's Mrs. Potts in name only.

FLO
Sometimes I think she keeps the boy's name just to defy
the old lady.

(ALAN's *car is heard approaching. It stops and the
car door slams.*)

MILLIE
(*Putting down her book*)
Hi, Alan! (*Jumps up, starts inside*) Oh, boy! I'm gonna
get my suit!

FLO
(*Calling after* MILLIE)
See if Madge is decent. (ALAN *comes on downstage, right*)
Good morning, Alan!

ALAN
Morning, Mrs. Owens . . . Miss Sydney.

> (ROSEMARY *doesn't bother to speak, usually affecting
> indifference to men.*)

MRS. POTTS
(*Coming back on from the passageway*)
Have you girls seen the handsome young man I've got
working for me?

ROSEMARY
I think it's a disgrace, his parading around, naked as an
Indian.

MRS. POTTS
(*Protectingly*)
I *told* him to take his shirt off.

FLO
Helen Potts, I wish you'd stop taking in all sorts of riffraff!

MRS. POTTS
He isn't riffraff. He's been to several colleges.

FLO
College—and he begs for breakfast!

MRS. POTTS
He's working for his breakfast! Alan, he said he knew you at the university.

ALAN
(*With no idea whom she's talking about*)
Who?

MILLIE
(*Coming out the front door*)
We going swimming, Alan?

ALAN
You bet.

FLO
Alan, why don't you go up and see Madge? Just call from the bottom of the stairs.

ALAN
(*Goes inside, calling*)
Hey, Delilah!

FLO
(*Seeing that* MILLIE *is about to follow* ALAN *inside*)
Millie!

(MILLIE *gets the idea that* MADGE *and* ALAN *are to be left alone. She sulks.*)

ROSEMARY
(*To* FLO, *confidentially*)
Do you think Alan's going to marry Madge?

FLO
(*She's usually a very truthful woman*)
I hadn't thought much about it.

MRS. POTTS
(*After a moment, drying her neck with handkerchief*)
It's so hot and still this time of year. When it gets this way
I'd welcome a good strong wind.

FLO
I'd rather wipe my brow than get blown away.

MRS. POTTS
(*Looking off at* HAL, *full of smiling admiration*)
Look at him lift that big old washtub like it was so much
tissue paper!

MRS. POTTS' MOTHER
(*Off stage, again*)
Helen! Helen!

MRS. POTTS
(*Patient but firm*)
I'm visiting Flo, Mama. You're all right. You don't need
me.

FLO
What did you feed him?

MRS. POTTS
Biscuits.

FLO
You went to all that trouble?

MRS. POTTS

He was *so* hungry. I gave him ham and eggs and all the hot coffee he could drink. Then he saw a piece of cherry pie in the icebox and he wanted that, too!

ROSEMARY
(*Laughs bawdily*)
Sounds to me like Mrs. Potts had herself a new boy friend!

MRS. POTTS
(*Rising, feeling injured*)
I don't think that's very funny.

FLO
Helen, come on. Sit down.

ROSEMARY
Shoot, Mrs. Potts, I'm just a tease.

FLO
Sit down, Helen.

MRS. POTTS
(*Still touchy*)
I *could* sit on my own porch, but I hate for the neighbors to see me there all alone.

(MADGE *and* ALAN *come out together,* MADGE *in her new dress. They march out hand in hand in a mock ceremony as though they were marching down the aisle.*)

ROSEMARY
(*Consolingly*)
Mrs. Potts, if I said anything to offend you . . .

FLO
(*Signals* ROSEMARY *to be quiet, points to* MADGE
and ALAN)

Bride and groom! Look, everybody! Bride and groom! (*To*
MADGE) How does it feel, Madge? (*Laughs at her uncon-
scious joke*) I mean the dress.

MADGE
(*Crossing to her mother*)

I love it, Mom, except it's a little tight in places.

MRS. POTTS
(*All eyes of admiration*)

Isn't Madge the pretty one!

ALAN
(*Turning to* MILLIE)

What are you reading, Millie?

MILLIE

The Ballad of the Sad Café by Carson McCullers. It's
wonderful!

ROSEMARY
(*Shocked*)

Good Lord, Mrs. Owens, you let your daughter read filthy
books like that?

FLO

Filthy?

ROSEMARY

Everyone in it is some sort of degenerate!

MILLIE

That's not so!

ROSEMARY

The D.A.R.'s had it banned from the public library.

MRS. POTTS
(*Eliminating herself from the argument*)
I don't read much.

FLO

Millie, give me that book!

MILLIE
(*Tenaciously*)

No!

ALAN

Mrs. Owens, I don't wanta interfere, but that book is on the reading list at college. For the course in the modern novel.

FLO
(*Full of confusion*)
Oh, dear! What's a person to believe?

(MILLIE *takes the book from* FLO. ALAN's *word about such matters is apparently final.*)

ROSEMARY

Well, those college professors don't have any morals!

(MILLIE *and* ALAN *shake hands.*)

FLO

Where Millie comes by her tastes, I'll never know.

MADGE
(*As* FLO *inspects her dress*)
Some of the pictures she has over her bed *scare* me.

MILLIE
Those pictures are by Picasso, and he's a great artist.

MADGE
A woman with seven eyes. Very pretty.

MILLIE
(*Delivering her ultimatum*)
Pictures don't have to be *pretty!*

(*A sudden explosion from* MRS. POTTS' *backyard. The women are startled.*)

FLO
Helen!

MRS. POTTS
(*Jumping up, alarmed*)
I'll go see what it is.

FLO
Stay here! He must have had a gun!

VOICE OFF STAGE
Helen! Helen!

FLO
(*Grabbing* MRS. POTTS' *arm*)
Don't go over there, Helen! Your mother's old. She has to go soon anyway!

MRS. POTTS
(*Running off stage*)
Pshaw! I'm not afraid.

ALAN
(*Looking off at* HAL)
Who did that guy say he was?

(*No one hears* ALAN.)

MRS. POTTS
(*Coming back and facing* FLO)
I was a bad girl.

FLO
What *is* it, Helen?

MRS. POTTS
I threw the *new* bottle of cleaning fluid into the trash.

FLO
You're the limit! Come on, Madge, let's finish that dress.

(FLO *and* MADGE *go into the house.* ROSEMARY *looks at her watch and then goes into the house also.*)

MRS. POTTS
Come help me, Millie. The young man ran into the clothes-line.

(*She and* MILLIE *hurry off stage.* ALAN *stands alone, trying to identify* HAL *who comes on from* MRS. POTTS'. HAL *is bare-chested now, wearing his T-shirt wrapped about his neck.* ALAN *finally recognizes him and is overjoyed at seeing him.*)

ALAN

Where did *you* come from?

HAL
(*Loud and hearty*)

Kid!

ALAN

Hal Carter!

HAL

I was comin' over to see you a little later.

ALAN
(*Recalling some intimate roughhouse greeting from
their college days*)

How's the old outboard motor?

HAL
(*With the eagerness of starting a game*)

Want a ride?

ALAN
(*Springing to* HAL, *clasping his legs around* HAL's
waist, hanging by one hand wrapped about HAL's
*neck, as though riding some sort of imagined ma-
chine*)

Gassed up? (*With his fingers, he twists* HAL's *nose as if it
were a starter.* HAL *makes the sputtering noise of an outboard
motor and swings* ALAN *about the stage,* ALAN *holding on
like a bronco-buster. They laugh uproariously together*) Ahoy,
brothers! Who's winkin', blinkin', and stinkin'?

(ALAN *drops to the ground, both of them still laughing uproariously with the recall of carefree, college
days.*)

HAL

That used to wake the whole damn fraternity!

ALAN

The last time I saw you, you were on your way to Hollywood to become a movie hero.

HAL

(*With a shrug of his shoulders*)

Oh, that!

ALAN

What do you mean, "Oh that"? Isn't that what I loaned you the hundred bucks for?

HAL

Sure, Seymour.

ALAN

Well, what happened?

HAL

(*He'd rather the subject had not been brought up*)

Things just didn't work out.

ALAN

I tried to warn you, Hal. Every year some talent scout promised screen tests to all the athletes.

HAL

Oh, I got the test okay! I was about to have a big career. They were gonna call me Brush Carter. How d'ya like that?

ALAN

Yeah?

HAL

Yah! They took a lotta pictures of me with my shirt off.
Real rugged. Then they dressed me up like the Foreign Le-
gion. Then they put me in a pair of tights—and they gave me
a big hat with a plume, and had me makin' with the sword
play. (*Pantomimes a duel*) Touché, mug! (*Returning the
sword to its scabbard*) It was real crazy!

ALAN

(*A little skeptical*)
Did they give you any lines to read?

HAL

Yah, that part went okay. It was my teeth.

ALAN

Your teeth?

HAL

Yah! Out there, you gotta have a certain kind of teeth
or they can't use you. Don't ask me why. This babe said
they'd have to pull all my teeth and give me new ones, so
naturally . . .

ALAN

Wait a minute. What babe?

HAL

The babe that got me the test. She wasn't a babe exactly.
She was kinda beat up—but not bad. (*He sees* ALAN's *crit-
ical eye*) Jesus, Seymour, a guy's gotta get along somehow.

ALAN

Uh-huh. What are you doing here?

HAL
(*A little hurt*)
Aren't you glad to see me?

ALAN
Sure, but fill me in.

HAL
Well—after I left Hollywood I took a job on a ranch in Nevada. You'da been proud of me, Seymour. In bed every night at ten, up every morning at six. No liquor—no babes. I saved up two hundred bucks!

ALAN
(*Holding out a hand*)
Oh! I'll take half.

HAL
Gee, Seymour, I wish I had it, but I got rolled.

ALAN
Rolled? *You?*

HAL
(*He looks to see that no one can overhear*)
Yeah, I was gonna hitchhike to Texas to get in a big oil deal. I got as far as Phoenix when two babes pull up in this big yellow convertible. And one of these dames slams on the brakes and hollers, "Get in, stud!" So I got in. Seymour, it was crazy. They had a shakerful of martinis right there in the car!

MRS. POTTS
(*Appears on her porch, followed by* MILLIE. MRS. POTTS *carries a cake*)
Oh, talking over old times? Millie helped me ice the cake.

HAL

Any more work, Mam?

MRS. POTTS

No. I feel I've been more than paid for the breakfast.

HAL

'Spose there's any place I could wash up?

MILLIE

We got a shower in the basement. Come on, I'll show you.

ALAN

(*Holding* HAL)

He'll be there in a minute. (MRS. POTTS *and* MILLIE *exit into the* OWENS *house*) Okay, so they had a shakerful of martinis!

HAL

And one of these babes was smokin' the weed!

ALAN

(*With vicarious excitement*)

Nothing like that ever happens to me! Go on!

HAL

Seymour, you wouldn't believe it, the things those two babes started doin' to me.

ALAN

Were they good-looking?

HAL

What do you care?

ALAN

Makes the story more interesting. Tell me what happened.

HAL

Well, you know *me,* Seymour. I'm an agreeable guy.

ALAN

Sure.

HAL

So when they parked in front of this tourist cabin, I said, "Okay, girls, if I gotta pay for the ride, this is the easiest way I know." (*He shrugs*) But, gee, they musta thought I was Superman.

ALAN

You mean—*both* of them?

HAL

Sure.

ALAN

Golly!

HAL

Then I said, "Okay, girls, the party's over—let's get goin.'" Then this dame on the weed, she sticks a gun in my back. She says, "This party's goin' on till *we* say it's over, Buck!" You'da thought she was Humphrey Bogart!

ALAN

Then what happened?

HAL

Finally I passed out! And when I woke up, the dames was gone and so was my two hundred bucks! I went to the police and they wouldn't believe me—they said my whole story was wishful thinking! How d'ya like *that*!

ALAN
(*Thinking it over*)

Mmmm.

HAL

Women are gettin' desperate, Seymour.

ALAN

Are they?

HAL

Well, that did it. Jesus, Seymour, what's a poor bastard like me ever gonna do?

ALAN

You don't sound like you had such a hard time.

HAL

I got thinking of you, Seymour, at school—how you always had things under control.

ALAN

Me?

HAL

Yah. Never cut classes — understood the lectures — took notes! (ALAN *laughs*) What's so funny?

ALAN

The hero of the campus, and he envied me!

HAL

Yah! Big hero, between the goal posts. You're the only guy in the whole fraternity ever treated me like a human being.

ALAN
(*With feeling for* HAL)

I know.

HAL

Those other snob bastards always watchin' to see which fork I used.

ALAN

You've got an inferiority complex. You imagined those things.

HAL

In a pig's eye!

ALAN
(*Delicately*)
What do you hear about your father?

HAL
(*Grave*)
It finally happened . . . before I left for Hollywood.

ALAN

What?

HAL
(*With a solemn hurt*)
He went on his last bender. The police scraped him up off the sidewalk. He died in jail.

ALAN
(*Moved*)
Gee, I'm sorry to hear that, Hal.

HAL
The old lady wouldn't even come across with the dough for the funeral. They had to bury him in Pauper's Row.

ALAN
What happened to the filling station?

HAL
He left it to me in his will, but the old lady was gonna have him declared insane so she could take over. I let her have it. Who cares?

ALAN
(*Rather depressed by* HAL's *story*)
Gee, Hal, I just can't believe people really do things like that.

HAL
Don't let *my* stories cloud up your rosy glasses.

ALAN
Why didn't you come to see me, when you got to town?

HAL
I didn't want to walk into your palatial mansion lookin' like a bum. I wanted to get some breakfast in my belly and pick up a little change.

ALAN
That wouldn't have made any difference.

HAL
I was hoping maybe you and your old man, between you, might fix me up with a job.

ALAN
What kind of a job, Hal?

HAL
What kinda jobs you got?

ALAN
What kind of job did you have in mind?

HAL
(*This is his favorite fantasy*)
Oh, something in a nice office where I can wear a tie and have a sweet little secretary and talk over the telephone about enterprises and things. (*As* ALAN *walks away skeptically*) I've always had the feeling, if I just had the chance, I could set the world on fire.

ALAN
Lots of guys have that feeling, Hal.

HAL
(*With some desperation*)
I gotta get some place in this world, Seymour. I *got* to.

ALAN
(*With a hand on* HAL's *shoulder*)
Take it easy.

HAL

This is a free country, and I got just as much rights as the next fellow. Why can't I get along?

ALAN

Don't worry, Hal. I'll help you out as much as I can. (MRS. POTTS *comes out the* OWENS' *back door*) Sinclair is hiring new men, aren't they, Mrs. Potts?

MRS. POTTS

Yes, Alan. Carey Hamilton needs a hundred new men for the pipeline.

HAL
(*Had dared to hope for more*)
Pipeline?

ALAN

If you wanta be president of the company, Hal, I guess you'll just have to work hard and be patient.

HAL
(*Clenching his fists together, so eager is he for patience*)
Yah. That's something I gotta learn. Patience!
(*He hurries inside the* OWENS' *back door now.*)

MRS. POTTS

I feel sorry for young men today.

ROSEMARY
(*Coming out the front door, very proud of the new outfit she is wearing, a fall suit and an elaborate hat*)
Is this a private party I'm crashin'?

MRS. POTTS
(*With some awe of* ROSEMARY's *finery*)
My, you're dressed up!

ROSEMARY
'S my new fall outfit. Got it in Kansas City. Paid twenty-two-fifty for the hat.

MRS. POTTS
You schoolteachers do have nice things.

ROSEMARY
And don't have to ask anybody when we wanta get 'em, either.

FLO
(*Coming out back door with* MADGE)
Be here for lunch today, Rosemary?

ROSEMARY
No. There's a welcome-home party down at the hotel. Lunch and bridge for the new girls on the faculty.

MADGE
Mom, can't I go swimming, too?

FLO
Who'll fix lunch? I've got a million things to do.

MADGE
It wouldn't kill Millie if she ever did any cooking.

FLO
No, but it might kill the rest of us.

(*Now we hear the voices of* IRMA KRONKITE *and* CHRISTINE SCHOENWALDER, *who are coming by for* ROSEMARY. *They think it playful to call from a distance.*)

IRMA

Rosemary! Let's get going, girl! (*As they come into sight,* IRMA *turns to* CHRISTINE) You'll love Rosemary Sydney. She's a peck of fun! Says the craziest things.

ROSEMARY
(*With playful suspiciousness*)
What're you saying about me, Irma Kronkite?

(*They run to hug each other like eager sisters who had not met in a decade.*)

IRMA

Rosemary Sydney!

ROSEMARY
Irma Kronkite! How was your vacation?

IRMA

I worked like a slave. But I had fun, too. I don't care if I *never* get that Masters. I'm not going to be a slave *all* my life.

CHRISTINE
(*Shyly*)
She's been telling me about all the wicked times she had in New York—and *not* at Teachers College, if I mav add.

IRMA
(*To* ROSEMARY)
Kid, this is Christine Schoenwalder, taking Mabel Fremont's
place in Feminine Hygiene. (ROSEMARY *and* CHRISTINE *shake
hands*) Been a hot summer, Mrs. Owens?

FLO
The worst I can remember.

MRS. POTTS
(*As* ROSEMARY *brings* CHRISTINE *up on porch*)
Delighted to know you, Christine. Welcome back, Irma.

IRMA
Are you working now, Madge?

MADGE
Yes.

FLO
(*Taking over for* MADGE)
Yes, Madge has been working downtown this summer—
just to keep busy. (*Now* HAL *and* MILLIE *burst out the
kitchen door, engaged in a noisy and furious mock fist-fight.*
HAL *is still bare-chested, his T-shirt still around his neck, and
the sight of him is something of a shock to the ladies*) Why,
when did he . . .

ALAN
(*Seizing* HAL *for an introduction*)
Mrs. Owens, this is my friend, Hal Carter. Hal is a fra-
ternity brother.

MRS. POTTS
(*Nudging* FLO)
What did I tell you, Flo?

FLO
(*Stunned*)
Fraternity brother! Really? (*Making the best of it*) Any
friend of Alan's is a friend of ours.

(*She offers* HAL *her hand.*)

HAL
Glad to make your acquaintance, Mam.

ALAN
(*Embarrassed for him*)
Hal, don't you have a shirt?

HAL
It's all sweaty, Seymour.

(ALAN *nudges him.* HAL *realizes he has said the
wrong thing and reluctantly puts on the T-shirt.*)

ROSEMARY
(*Collecting* IRMA *and* CHRISTINE)
Girls, we better get a hustle on.

CHRISTINE
(*To* IRMA)
Tell them about what happened in New York, kid.

IRMA
(*The center of attention*)
I went to the Stork Club!

ROSEMARY

How did *you* get to the Stork Club?

IRMA

See, there was this fellow in my Educational Statistics
class . . .

ROSEMARY
(*Continuing the joke*)
I *knew* there was a *man* in it.

IRMA

Now, girl! It was nothing serious. He was just a good
sport, that's all. We made a bet that the one who made the
lowest grade on the *final* had to take the other to the Stork
Club—and *I* lost!

(*The teachers go off noisily laughing, as* FLO *and*
MRS. POTTS *watch them.*)

ALAN
(*Calling to* HAL, *at back of stage playing with*
MILLIE)
Wanta go swimming, Hal? I've got extra trunks in the car.

HAL

Why not?

MRS. POTTS
(*In a private voice*)
Flo, let's ask the young man on the picnic. He'd be a date
for Millie.

FLO

That's right, but . . .

MRS. POTTS
(*Taking it upon herself*)
Young man, Flo and I are having a picnic for the young
people. You come, too, and be an escort for Millie.

HAL
Picnic?

MRS. POTTS
Yes.

HAL
I don't think it's right, me bargin' in this way.

MRS. POTTS
Nonsense. A picnic's no fun without lots and lots of young
people.

ALAN
(*Bringing* HAL *down center*)
Hal, I want you to meet Madge.

MADGE
Oh, we've met already. That is, we *saw* each other.

HAL
Yah, we saw each other.

ALAN
(*To* MADGE)
Hal sees every pretty girl.

MADGE
(*Pretending to protest*)
Alan.

ALAN

Well, you're the prettiest girl in town, aren't you? (*To*
HAL) The Chamber of Commerce voted her Queen of Neewollah last year.

HAL

I don't dig.

MILLIE

She was Queen of Neewollah. Neewollah is Halloween
spelled backwards.

MRS. POTTS
(*Joining in*)

Every year they have a big coronation ceremony in Memo-
rial Hall, with all kinds of artistic singing and dancing.

MILLIE

Madge had to sit through the whole ceremony till they put
a crown on her head.

HAL
(*Impressed*)

Yah?

MADGE

I got awfully tired.

MILLIE

The Kansas City *Star* ran color pictures in their Sunday
magazine.

MADGE

Everyone expected me to get real conceited, but I didn't.

HAL

You didn't?

MILLIE

It'd be pretty hard to get conceited about *those* pictures.

MADGE
(*Humorously*)
The color got blurred and my mouth was printed right in the middle of my forehead.

HAL
(*Sympathetic*)
Gee, that's too bad.

MADGE
(*Philosophically*)
Things like that are bound to happen.

MILLIE
(*To* HAL)
I'll race you to the car.

HAL
(*Starting off with* MILLIE)
Isn't your sister goin' with us?

MILLIE

Madge has to cook lunch.

HAL

Do you mean *she cooks*?

MILLIE

Sure! Madge cooks and sews and does all those things that women do.

> (*They race off,* MILLIE *getting a head start through the gate and* HAL *scaling the fence to get ahead of her.*)

FLO
> (*In a concerned voice*)

Alan!

ALAN

Yes?

FLO

How did a boy like him get into college?

ALAN

On a football scholarship. He made a spectacular record in a little high school down in Arkansas.

FLO

But a fraternity! Don't those boys have a little more . . . breeding?

ALAN

I guess they're *supposed* to, but fraternities like to pledge big athletes — for the publicity. And Hal could have been All-American . . .

MRS. POTTS
> (*Delighted*)

All-American!

ALAN

. . . if he'd only studied.

FLO

But how did the other boys feel about him?

ALAN

(*Reluctantly*)

They didn't like him, Mrs. Owens. They were pretty rough on him. Every time he came into a room, the other fellows seemed to *bristle*. I didn't like him either, at first. Then we shared a room and I got to know him better. Hal's really a nice guy. About the best friend I ever had.

FLO

(*More to the point*)

Is he wild?

ALAN

Oh—not really. He just . . .

FLO

Does he drink?

ALAN

A little. (*Trying to minimize*) Mrs. Owens, Hal pays attention to me. I'll see he behaves.

FLO

I wouldn't want anything to happen to Millie.

MADGE

Millie can take care of herself. You pamper her.

FLO

Maybe I do. Come on, Helen. (*As she and* MRS. POTTS
go in through the back door) Oh, dear, why can't things be
simple?

ALAN

(*After* FLO *and* MRS. POTTS *leave*)
Madge, I'm sorry I have to go back to school this fall. It's
Dad's idea.

MADGE

I thought it was.

ALAN

Really, Madge, Dad likes you very much. I'm sure he does.

(*But* ALAN *himself doesn't sound convinced.*)

MADGE

Well—he's always very polite.

ALAN

I'll miss you, Madge.

MADGE

There'll be lots of pretty girls at college.

ALAN

Honestly, Madge, my entire four years I never found a girl
I liked.

MADGE

I don't believe that.

ALAN

It's true. They're all so affected, if you wanted a date with
them you had to call them a month in advance.

MADGE

Really?

ALAN

Madge, it's hard to say, but I honestly never believed that
a girl like you could care for me.

MADGE
(*Touched*)

Alan . . .

ALAN

I—I hope you do care for me, Madge.

(*He kisses her.*)

HAL

(*Comes back on stage somewhat apologetically. He
is worried about something and tries to get* ALAN's
attention)

Hey, Seymour . . .

ALAN
(*Annoyed*)

What's the matter, Hal? Can't you stand to see anyone
else kiss a pretty girl?

HAL

What the hell, Seymour!

ALAN
                    (*An excuse to be angry*)
Hal, will you watch your language!

MADGE

Alan! It's all right.

HAL

I'm sorry.
          (*Beckons* ALAN *to him.*)

ALAN
                    (*Crossing to him*)
What's the trouble?

          (MADGE *walks away, sensing that* HAL *wants to talk
          privately.*)

HAL

Look, Seymour, I—I never been on a picnic.

ALAN

What're you talking about? Everybody's been on a picnic.

HAL

Not me. When I was a kid, I was too busy shooting craps
or stealing milk bottles.

ALAN

Well, there's a first time for everything.

HAL

I wasn't brought up proper like *you*. I won't know how to
act around all these *women*.

ALAN

Women aren't anything new in *your* life.

HAL

But these are—*nice* women. What if I say the wrong word
or maybe my stomach growls? I feel *funny*.

ALAN

You're a psycho!

HAL

OK, but if I do anything wrong, you gotta try to overlook
it.
> (*He runs off stage.* ALAN *laughs. Then* ALAN *returns
> to* MADGE.)

ALAN

We'll be by about five, Madge.

MADGE

OK.

ALAN
(*Beside her, tenderly*)

Madge, after we have supper tonight maybe you and I can
get away from the others and take a boat out on the river.

MADGE

All right, Alan.

ALAN

I want to see if you look *real* in the moonlight.

MADGE

Alan! Don't say that!

ALAN

Why? I don't care if you're real or not. You're the prettiest girl I ever saw.

MADGE

Just the same, I'm real.

(*As* ALAN *starts to kiss her, the noise of an automobile horn is heard.*)

HAL

(*Hollering lustily from off stage*)

Hey, Seymour—get the lead outa your pants!

(ALAN *goes off, irritated.* MADGE *watches them as they drive away. She waves to them.*)

FLO

(*Inside*)

Madge! Come on inside now.

MADGE

All right, Mom.

(*As she starts in, there is a train whistle in the distance.* MADGE *hears it and stands listening.*)

CURTAIN

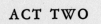

ACT TWO

ACT TWO

It is late afternoon, the same day. The sun is beginning to set and fills the atmosphere with radiant orange. When the curtain goes up, MILLIE is on the porch alone. She has permitted herself to "dress up" and wears a becoming, feminine dress in which she cannot help feeling a little strange. She is quite attractive. Piano music can be heard off stage, somewhere past MRS. POTTS' house, and MILLIE stands listening to it for a moment. Then she begins to sway to the music and in a moment is dancing a strange, impromptu dance over the porch and yard. The music stops suddenly and MILLIE's mood is broken. She rushes upstage and calls off, left.

MILLIE

Don't quit now, Ernie! (*She cannot hear* ERNIE's *reply*) Huh? (MADGE *enters from kitchen.* MILLIE *turns to* MADGE) Ernie's waiting for the rest of the band to practice. They're going to play out at the park tonight.

MADGE

(*Crossing to center and sitting on chair*)
I don't know why you couldn't have helped us in the kitchen.

MILLIE

(*Lightly, giving her version of the sophisticated belle*)
I had to dress for the ball.

65

MADGE

I had to make the potato salad and stuff the eggs and make three dozen bread-and-butter sandwiches.

MILLIE
(*In a very affected accent*)

I had to *bathe*—and dust my limbs with powder—and slip into my frock . . .

MADGE

Did you clean out the bathtub?

MILLIE

Yes, I cleaned out the bathtub. (*She becomes very self-conscious*) Madge, how do I look? Now tell me the truth.

MADGE

You look very pretty.

MILLIE

I feel sorta funny.

MADGE

You can have the dress if you want it.

MILLIE

Thanks. (*A pause*) Madge, how do you talk to boys?

MADGE

Why, you just talk, silly.

MILLIE

How d'ya think of things to say?

MADGE

I don't know. You just say whatever comes into your head.

MILLIE

Supposing nothing ever comes into my head?

MADGE

You talked with him all right this morning.

MILLIE

But now I've got a *date* with him, and it's *different*!

MADGE

You're crazy.

MILLIE

I think he's a big show-off. You should have seen him this morning on the high diving board. He did real graceful swan dives, and a two and a half gainer, and a back flip—and kids stood around clapping. He just ate it up.

MADGE
(*Her mind elsewhere*)
I think I'll paint my toenails tonight and wear sandals.

MILLIE

And he was braggin' all afternoon how he used to be a deep-sea diver off Catalina Island.

MADGE

Honest?

MILLIE

And he says he used to make hundreds of dollars doin' parachute jumps out of a balloon. Do you believe it?

MADGE

I don't see why not.

MILLIE

You never hear Alan bragging that way.

MADGE

Alan never jumped out of a balloon.

MILLIE

Madge, I think he's girl crazy.

MADGE

You think every boy you see is something horrible.

MILLIE

Alan took us into the Hi Ho for Cokes and there was a gang of girls in the back booth — Juanita Badger and her gang. (MADGE *groans at hearing this name*) When they saw him, they started giggling and tee-heeing and saying all sorts of crazy things. Then Juanita Badger comes up to me and whispers, "He's the cutest thing I ever saw." Is he, Madge?

MADGE

(*Not willing to go overboard*)

I certainly wouldn't say he was "the cutest thing I ever *saw.*"

MILLIE

Juanita Badger's an old floozy. She sits in the back row at the movie so the guys that come in will see her and sit with her. One time she and Rubberneck Krauss were asked by the management to leave—and thev weren't just kissin', either!

MADGE
(*Proudly*)
I never even speak to Juanita Badger.

MILLIE
Madge, do you think he'll like me?

MADGE
Why ask me all these questions? You're supposed to be
the smart one.

MILLIE
I don't really care. I just wonder.

FLO
(*Coming out of kitchen*)
Now I tell myself I've got two beautiful daughters.

MILLIE
(*Embarrassed*)
Be quiet, Mom!

FLO
Doesn't Millie look pretty, Madge?

MADGE
When she isn't picking her nose.

FLO
Madge! (*To* MILLIE) She doesn't want anyone to be
pretty but her.

MILLIE
You're just saying I'm pretty because you're my mom.
People we love are always pretty, but people who're pretty
to begin with, everybody loves *them*.

FLO

Run over and show Helen Potts how nice you look.

MILLIE
(*In a wild parody of herself*)
Here comes Millie Owens, the great beauty of all time!
Be prepared to swoon when you see her!

(*She climbs up over the side of* MRS. POTTS' *porch
and disappears.*)

FLO
(*Sits on chair on porch*)
Whatever possessed me to let Helen Potts ask that young
hoodlum to take Millie on the picnic?

MADGE

Hal?

FLO

Yes, Hal, or whatever his name is. He left every towel in
the bathroom black as dirt. He left the seat up, too.

MADGE

It's not going to hurt anyone just to be nice to him.

FLO

If there's any drinking tonight, you put a stop to it.

MADGE

I'm not going to be a wet blanket.

FLO

If the boys feel they have to have a few drinks, there's
nothing you can do about it, but you can keep Millie from
taking any.

MADGE

She wouldn't pay any attention to me.

FLO
(*Changing the subject*)
You better be getting dressed. And don't spend the whole evening admiring yourself in the mirror.

MADGE

Mom, don't make fun of me.

FLO
You shouldn't object to being kidded if it's well meant.

MADGE
It seems like—when I'm looking in the mirror that's the only way I can prove to myself I'm alive.

FLO
Madge! You puzzle me.

(*The three schoolteachers come on, downstage right, making a rather tired return from their festivity. After their high-spirited exit in Act One, their present mood seems glum, as though they had expected from the homecoming some fulfillment that had not been realized.*)

IRMA
We've brought home your wayward girl, Mrs. Owens!

FLO
(*Turning from* MADGE)
Hello, girls! Have a nice party?

IRMA

It wasn't a real party. Each girl paid for her own lunch.
Then we played bridge all afternoon. (*Confidentially to* ROSE-
MARY) I get tired playing bridge.

FLO

Food's good at the hotel, isn't it?

IRMA

Not very. But they serve it to you nice, with honest-to-
goodness napkins. Lord, I hate paper napkins!

CHRISTINE

I had a French-fried pork chop and it was mostly fat.
What'd you girls have?

ROSEMARY

I had the stuffed peppers.

IRMA

I had the Southern-fried chicken.

CHRISTINE

Linda Sue Breckenridge had pot roast of veal and there
was only one little hunk of meat in it. All we girls at her
table made her call the waiter and complain.

ROSEMARY

Well, I should hope so!

IRMA

Good for you! (*There is a pause*) I thought by this time
someone might have noticed my new dress.

ROSEMARY

I was going to say something, kid, and then I . . . uh . . .

IRMA

Remember that satin-back crepe I had last year?

ROSEMARY

Don't tell me!

IRMA

Mama remodeled it for me while I was at Columbia. I feel like I had a brand-new outfit. (*Smarting*) But nobody said anything all afternoon!

CHRISTINE

It's—chic.

IRMA

(*This soothes* IRMA *a bit and she beams. But now there is an awkward pause wherein no one can think of any more to say*)

Well — we better run along, Christine. Rosemary has a date. (*To* ROSEMARY) We'll come by for you in the morning. Don't be late.

(*She goes upstage and waits at the gate for* CHRIS-TINE.)

CHRISTINE

(*Crossing to* ROSEMARY)

Girl, I want to tell you, in one afternoon I feel I've known you my whole life.

ROSEMARY

(*With assurance of devotion*)

I look upon you as an old friend already.

CHRISTINE
(*Overjoyed*)
Aw . . .

ROSEMARY
(*As* CHRISTINE *and* IRMA *go off*)
Good-bye, girls!

FLO
(*To* ROSEMARY)
What time's Howard coming by?

ROSEMARY
Any minute now.

MADGE
Mom, is there any hot water?

FLO
You'll have to see.

MADGE
(*Crosses to door, then turns to* ROSEMARY)
Miss Sydney, would you mind terribly if I used some of
your Shalimar?

ROSEMARY
Help yourself!

MADGE
Thanks.
(*She goes inside.*)

ROSEMARY
Madge thinks too much about the boys, Mrs. Owens.

FLO
(*Disbelieving*)

Madge?

(*The conversation is stopped by the excited entrance
of* MRS. POTTS *from her house. She is followed by*
MILLIE *who carries another cake.*)

MRS. POTTS

It's a *miracle*, that's what it is! I never knew Millie could
look so pretty. It's just like a movie I saw once with Betty
Grable—or was it Lana Turner? Anyway, she played the part
of a secretary to some very important business man. She wore
glasses and did her hair real plain and men didn't pay any
attention to her at all. Then one day she took off her glasses
and her boss wanted to marry her right away! Now all the
boys are going to fall in love with Millie!

ROSEMARY

Millie have a date tonight?

FLO

Yes, I'm sorry to say.

MRS. POTTS

Why, Flo!

ROSEMARY

Who is he, Millie? Tell your Aunt Rosemary.

MILLIE

Hal.

ROSEMARY

Who?

FLO

The young man over at Helen's turned out to be a friend of Alan's.

ROSEMARY

Oh, *him*!

(MILLIE *exits into kitchen.*)

FLO

Helen, have you gone to the trouble of baking another cake?

MRS. POTTS

An old lady like me, if she wants any attention from the young men on a picnic, all she can do is bake a cake!

FLO
(*Rather reproving*)

Helen Potts!

MRS. POTTS

I feel sort of excited, Flo. I think we plan picnics just to give ourselves an excuse—to let something thrilling happen in our lives.

FLO

Such as what?

MRS. POTTS

I don't know.

MADGE
(*Bursting out the door*)

Mom, Millie makes me furious! Every time she takes a bath, she fills the whole tub. There isn't any hot water at all.

FLO

You should have thought of it earlier.

ROSEMARY

(*Hears* HOWARD's *car drive up and stop*)

It's him! It's him!

MRS. POTTS

Who? Oh, it's Howard. Hello, Howard!

ROSEMARY

(*Sitting down again*)

If he's been drinking, I'm not going out with him.

HOWARD

(*As he comes on through gate*)

Howdy, ladies.

(HOWARD *is a small, thin man, rapidly approaching middle age. A small-town businessman, he wears a permanent smile of greeting which, most of the time, is pretty sincere.*)

FLO

Hello, Howard.

HOWARD

You sure look nice, Rosemary.

ROSEMARY

(*Her tone of voice must tell a man she is independent of him*)

Seems to me you might have left your coat on.

HOWARD

Still too darn hot, even if it is September. Good evening, Madge.

MADGE

Hi, Howard.

FLO

How are things over in Cherryvale, Howard?

HOWARD

Good business. Back to school and everybody buying.

FLO

When business is good, it's good for everyone.

MILLIE

(*Comes out of kitchen, stands shyly behind* HOWARD)
Hi, Howard!

HOWARD

(*Turning around, making a discovery*)
Hey, Millie's a good-lookin' kid. I never realized it before.

MILLIE

(*Crossing to* FLO, *apprehensive*)
Mom, what time did the fellows say they'd be here?

FLO

At five-thirty. You've asked me a dozen times. (*There is a sound of approaching automobiles, and* FLO *looks off stage, right*) Alan's brought *both* cars!

(MILLIE *runs into the house.*)

MRS. POTTS
(*To* FLO)

Some day *you'll* be riding around in that big Cadillac,
Lady-bug.

ALAN
(*Coming on from right*)

Everyone ready?

FLO

Come sit down, Alan.

ROSEMARY
(*Like a champion hostess*)

The more the merrier!

ALAN

I brought both cars. I thought we'd let Hal and Millie
bring the baskets out in the Ford. Hal's parking it now. (*To*
MADGE, *who is sitting up on* MRS. POTTS' *porch railing*)
Hello, Beautiful!

MADGE

Hello, Alan!

ALAN
(*Calling off stage*)

Come on, Hal.

FLO

Is he a careful driver, Alan?

> (*This question does not get answered.* HAL *comes
> running on, tugging uncomfortably at the shoulders
> of his jacket and hollering in a voice that once filled
> the locker rooms.*)

HAL

Hey, Seymour! Hey, I'm a big man, Seymour. I'm a lot huskier than you are. I can't wear your jacket.

ALAN

Then take it off.

MRS. POTTS

Yes. I like to see a man comfortable.

HAL
(*With a broad smile of total confidence*)
I never could wear another fellow's clothes. See, I'm pretty big through the shoulders. (*He demonstrates the fact*) I should have all my clothes tailor-made.

> (*He now swings his arms in appreciation of their new freedom.* MRS. POTTS *is admiring, the other women speculative.*)

ALAN
(*Wanting to get over the formalities*)
Hey—uh—Hercules, you've met Mrs. Owens . . .

HAL

Sure!
> (FLO *nods at him.*)

ALAN

. . . and I believe you met Mrs. Potts this morning.

HAL
(*Throwing his arms around her*)
Oh, she's my best girl!

MRS. POTTS
(*Giggling like a girl*)
I baked a Lady Baltimore cake!

HAL
(*Expansively, as though making an announcement of
public interest*)
This little lady, she took pity on me when I was practically starving. I ran into some hard luck when I was travelin'. Some characters robbed me of every cent I had.

ALAN
(*Interrupting*)
And — er — this is Rosemary Sydney, Hal. Miss Sydney teaches shorthand and typing in the local high school.

ROSEMARY
(*Offering her hand*)
Yes, I'm an old-maid schoolteacher.

HAL
(*With unnecessary earnestness*)
I have every respect for schoolteachers, Mam. It's a lotta hard work and not much pay.
(ROSEMARY *cannot decide whether or not this is a
compliment.*)

ALAN
And this is Howard Bevans, Hal. Mr. Bevans is a friend of Miss Sydney.

HOWARD
(*As they shake hands*)
I run a little shop over in Cherryvale. Notions, novelties and school supplies. You and Alan drive over some time and get acquainted.

(MILLIE *enters and stands on the porch, pretending to be nonchalant and at ease.*)

HAL
(*To* HOWARD, *earnestly*)

Sir, we'll come over as soon as we can fit it into our schedule. (*He spies* MILLIE) Hey kid! (*He does an elaborate imitation of a swan dive and lands beside her on the porch*) You got a little more tan today, didn't you? (*He turns to the others*) You folks shoulda seen Millie this morning. She did a fine jack-knife off the high diving board!

MILLIE
(*Breaking away, sitting on steps*)
Cut it out!

HAL

What'sa matter, kid? Think I'm snowin' you under? (*Back to the whole group*) I wouldn't admit this to many people, but she does a jack-knife almost as good as me! (*Realizes that this sounds bragging so goes on to explain*) You see, I was diving champion on the West Coast, so I know what I'm talking about!

(*He laughs to reassure himself and sits beside* MILLIE *on doorstep.*)

FLO
(*After a moment*)
Madge, you should be getting dressed.

ALAN
Go on upstairs and get beautiful for us.

MADGE

Mom, can I wear my new dress?

FLO

No. I made you that dress to save for dances this fall.

(*The attention returns now to* HAL, *and* MADGE *continues to sit, unnoticed, watching him.*)

ROSEMARY
(*To* HAL)

Where'd you get those boots?

HAL

I guess maybe I should apologize for the way I look. But you see, those characters I told you about made off with all my clothes, too.

MRS. POTTS

What a pity!

HAL

You see, I didn't want you folks to think you were associatin' with a bum.

(*He laughs uncomfortably.*)

MRS. POTTS
(*Intuitively, she says what is needed to save his ego*)

Clothes don't make the man.

HAL

That's what I tell myself, Mam.

FLO

Is your mother taken care of, Helen?

MRS. POTTS

Yes, Flo. I've got a baby sitter for her.

(*All laugh.*)

FLO

Then let's start packing the baskets.

(*She goes into kitchen.* MRS. POTTS *starts after her, but* HAL's *story holds her and she sits down again.*)

HAL

(*Continuing his explanation to Rosemary*)
See, Mam, my old man left me these boots when he died.

ROSEMARY

(*Impishly*)
That all he left you—just a pair of boots?

HAL

He said, "Son, the man of the house needs a pair of boots 'cause he's gotta do a lot of kickin'.

> Your wages all are spent.
> The landlord wants his rent.
> You go to your woman for solace,
> And she fills you fulla torment."

(HAL *smiles and explains proudly*) That's a little poem he made up. He says, "Son, there'll be times when the only thing you got to be proud of is the fact you're a man. So wear your boots so people can hear you comin', and keep your fists doubled up so they'll know you mean business when you get there." (*He laughs*) My old man, he was a corker!

ALAN
(*Laughing*)
Hal's always so shy of people before he meets them. Then
you can't keep him still!

(*Suddenly* HAL's *eye catches* MADGE, *perched on* MRS.
POTTS' *porch.*)

HAL
Hi!

MADGE
Hi!

(*Now they both look away from each other, a little
guiltily.*)

HOWARD
What line of business you in, Son?

HAL
(*He begins to expand with importance*)
I'm about to enter the oil business, sir.

(*He sits on the chair, center stage.*)

HOWARD
Oh!

HAL
You see, while my old man was no aristocratic millionaire
or anything, he had some very important friends who were
very big men—in their own way. One of them wanted me to
take a position with this oil company down in Texas, but...

ALAN
(*Matter-of-factly*)
Dad and I have found a place for Hal on the pipeline.

HAL

Gee, Seymour, I think you oughta let *me* tell the story.

ALAN
(*Knowing he might as well let* HAL *go on*)
Sorry, Hal.

HAL
(*With devout earnestness to all*)
You see, I've decided to start in from the very bottom,
'cause that way I'll learn things lots better—even if I don't
make much money for a while.

MRS. POTTS
(*Comes through again*)
Money isn't everything.

HAL
That's what I tell myself, Mam. Money isn't everything.
I've learned that much. And I sure do appreciate Alan and
his old . . . (*Thinks a moment and substitutes* father *for* man)
father . . . giving me this opportunity.

MRS. POTTS
I think that's wonderful.
(*She has every faith in him.*)

HOWARD
It's a good business town. A young man can go far.

HAL
Sir! I intend to go *far*.

ROSEMARY
(*Her two-bits' worth*)
A young man, coming to town, he's gotta be a good mixer.

MRS. POTTS

Wouldn't it be nice if he could join the Country Club and play golf?

ALAN

He won't be able to afford that.

ROSEMARY

The bowling team's a rowdy gang.

MRS. POTTS

And there's a young men's Bible class at the Baptist Church.

(HAL's *head has been spinning with these plans for his future. Now he reassures them.*)

HAL

Oh, I'm gonna join clubs and go to church and do all those things.

FLO
(*Coming out of the kitchen*)

Madge! Are you still here?

MADGE
(*Running across to the front door of her own house*)

If everyone will pardon me, I'll get dressed.

(*She goes inside.*)

FLO

It's about time.

ALAN
(*Calling after* MADGE)

Hurry it up, will you, Delilah?

MILLIE

You oughta see the way Madge primps. She uses about six kinds of face cream and dusts herself all over with powder, and rubs perfume underneath her ears to make her real mysterious. It takes her half an hour just to get her lipstick on. She won't be ready for hours.

FLO

Come on, Helen. Alan, we'll need a man to help us chip the ice and put the baskets in the car.

(MRS. POTTS *goes inside.*)

HAL
(*Generously*)

I'll help you, Mam.

FLO
(*She simply cannot accept him*)

No, thank you. Alan won't mind.

ALAN
(*To* HAL *as he leaves*)

Mind your manners, Hal.

(*He and* FLO *start in.*)

MILLIE
(*Uncertain how to proceed with* HAL *on her own, she runs to* FLO)

Mom!

FLO

Millie, show the young man your drawings.

MILLIE
(*To* HAL)

Wanta see my art?

HAL

You mean to tell me you can draw pictures?

MILLIE
(*Gets her sketch book and shows it to* HAL. FLO *and*
ALAN *go inside*)

That's Mrs. Potts.

HAL
(*Impressed*)

Looks just like her.

MILLIE

I just love Mrs. Potts. When I go to heaven, I expect
everyone to be just like her.

HAL

Hey, kid, wanta draw me?

MILLIE

Well, I'll try.

HAL

I had a job as a model once. (*Strikes a pose*) How's this?
(MILLIE *shakes her head*) Here's another. (*Sits on stump
in another pose*) Okay?

MILLIE

Why don't you just try to look natural?

HAL

Gee, that's hard.

(*But he shakes himself into a natural pose finally.* MILLIE *starts sketching him.* ROSEMARY *and* HOWARD *sit together on the doorstep. The sun now is beginning to set, filling the stage with an orange glow that seems almost aflame.*)

ROSEMARY
(*Grabs* HOWARD's *arm*)
Look at that sunset, Howard!

HOWARD
Pretty, isn't it?

ROSEMARY
That's the most flaming sunset I ever did see.

HOWARD
If you painted it in a picture, no one'd believe you.

ROSEMARY
It's like the daytime didn't want to end, isn't it?

HOWARD
(*Not fully aware of what she means*)
Oh—I don't know.

ROSEMARY
Like the daytime didn't wanta end, like it was gonna put up a big scrap and maybe set the world on fire—to keep the nighttime from creepin' on.

HOWARD

Rosemary . . . you're a poet.

HAL

(*As* MILLIE *sketches him he begins to relax and reflect on his life*)

You know, there comes a time in every man's life when he's gotta settle down. A little town like this, this is the place to settle down in, where people are easygoin' and sincere.

ROSEMARY

No, Howard, I don't think there ought to be any drinking, while Millie's here.

HAL

(*Turns at the mention of drink*)

What's that?

ROSEMARY

We were just talkin'.

HAL

(*Back to* MILLIE)

What'd you do this afternoon, kid?

MILLIE

Read a book.

HAL

(*Impressed*)

You mean, you read a *whole* book in one afternoon?

MILLIE

Sure. Hold still.

HAL

I'm a son of a gun. What was it about?

MILLIE

There wasn't much story. It's just the way you feel when you read it—kind of warm inside and sad and amused—all at the same time.

HAL

Yeah—sure. (*After a moment*) I wish I had more time to read books. (*Proudly*) That's what I'm gonna do when I settle down. I'm gonna read all the better books—and listen to all the better music. A man owes it to himself. (MILLIE *continues sketching*) I used to go with a girl who read books. She joined the Book-of-the-Month Club and they had her readin' books all the time! She wouldn't any more finish one book than they'd send her another!

ROSEMARY

(*As* HOWARD *walks off*)

Howard, where you goin'?

HOWARD

I'll be right back, Honey.

(ROSEMARY *follows him to gate and watches him while he is off stage.*)

HAL

(*As* MILLIE *hands him the sketch*)

Is that *me*? (*Admiring it*) I sure do admire people who are artistic. Can I keep it?

MILLIE

Sure. (*Shyly*) I write poetry, too. I've written poems I've never shown to a living soul.

HAL

Kid, I think you must be some sort of a genius.

ROSEMARY

(*Calling off to* HOWARD)

Howard, leave that bottle right where it is!

HAL

(*Jumps at the word* bottle)

Did she say "bottle"?

ROSEMARY

(*Coming down to* HAL)

He's been down to the hotel, buying bootleg whiskey off those good-for-nothing porters!

HOWARD

(*Coming back, holding out a bottle*)

Young man, maybe you'd like a swig of this.

HAL

Hot damn!

(*He takes a drink.*)

ROSEMARY

Howard, put that away.

HOWARD

Millie's not gonna be shocked if she sees someone take a drink. Are you, Millie?

MILLIE

Gosh, no!

ROSEMARY

What if someone'd come by and tell the School Board?
I'd lose my job quick as you can say Jack Robinson.

HOWARD

Who's gonna see you, Honey? Everyone in town's at the
park, havin' a picnic.

ROSEMARY

I don't care. Liquor's against the law in this state, and a
person oughta abide by the law. (*To* HAL) Isn't that what
you say, young fellow?

HAL
(*Eager to agree*)
Oh, sure! A person oughta abide by the law.

HOWARD

Here, Honey, have one.

ROSEMARY

No, Howard, I'm not gonna touch a drop.

HOWARD

Come on, Honey, have one little drink just for *me*.

ROSEMARY
(*Beginning to melt*)
Howard, you oughta be ashamed of yourself.

HOWARD
(*Innocent*)
I don't see why.

ROSEMARY

I guess I know why you want me to take a drink.

HOWARD

Now, Honey, that's not so. I just think you should have a good time like the rest of us. (*To* HAL) Schoolteachers gotta right to live. Isn't that what you say, young fella?

HAL

Sure, schoolteachers got a right to live.

ROSEMARY
(*Taking the bottle*)
Now, Millie, don't you tell any of the kids at school.

MILLIE

What do you take me for?

ROSEMARY
(*Looking around her*)
Anyone coming?

HOWARD

Coast is clear.

ROSEMARY
(*Takes a hearty drink, and makes a lugubrious face*)
Whew! I want some water!

HOWARD

Millie, why don't you run in the house and get us some?

ROSEMARY

Mrs. Owens'd suspect something. I'll get a drink from the hydrant!

(*She runs off to* MRS. POTTS' *yard.*)

HOWARD

Millie, my girl, I'd like to offer *you* one, but I s'pose your old lady'd raise Ned.

MILLIE

What Mom don't know won't hurt her!

(*She reaches for the bottle.*)

HAL
(*Grabs the bottle first*)
No, kid. You lay off the stuff!

(*He takes another drink*)

ROSEMARY
(*Calling from off stage*)
Howard, come help me! I see a snake!

HOWARD

You go, Millie. She don't see no snake. (MILLIE *goes off. As* HAL *takes another drink, he sees a light go on in* MADGE's *window.* HOWARD *follows* HAL's *gaze*) Look at her there, powdering her arms. You know, every time I come over here I look forward just to seein' her. I tell myself, "Bevans, old boy, you can look at that all you want, but you couldn't touch it with a ten-foot pole."

HAL
(*With some awe of her*)
She's the kind of girl a guy's gotta *respect*.

HOWARD

Look at her, putting lipstick on that cute kisser. Seems to me, when the good Lord made a girl as pretty as she is, he did it for a reason, and it's about time she found out what that reason is. (*He gets an idea*) Look, son, if you're agonizin', I know a couple of girls down at the hotel.

HAL

Thanks, but I've given up that sorta thing.

HOWARD

I think that's a very fine attitude.

HAL

Besides, I never had to pay for it.

ROSEMARY
(*Entering, followed by* MILLIE)

Lord, I thought I was going to faint!

MILLIE
(*Laughing at* ROSEMARY's *excitability*)

It was just a piece of garden hose.

ROSEMARY
(*Regarding the two men suspiciously*)

What're you two talking about?

HOWARD

Talkin' about the weather, Honey. Talkin' about the weather.

ROSEMARY

I bet.

MILLIE
(*Seeing* MADGE *in the window*)
Hey, Madge, why don't you charge admission?

(MADGE'S *curtains close.*)

ROSEMARY
Shoot! When I was a girl I was just as good-looking as she is!

HOWARD
Of course you were, Honey.

ROSEMARY
(*Taking the bottle*)
I had boys callin' me all the time. But if my father had ever caught me showing off in front of the window he'd have tanned me with a razor strap. (*Takes a drink*) Cause I was brought up strict by a God-fearing man.

(*Takes another.*)

MILLIE
(*Music has started in the background*)
Hey, hit it, Ernie! (*Explaining to* HAL) It's Ernie Higgins and his Happiness Boys. They play at all the dances around here.

ROSEMARY
(*Beginning to sway rapturously*)
Lord, I like that music! Come dance with me, Howard.

HOWARD
Honey, I'm no good at dancin'.

ROSEMARY

That's just what you menfolks tell yourselves to get out of it. (*Turns to* MILLIE) Come dance with me, Millie!

> (*She pulls* MILLIE *up onto the porch and they push the chairs out of the way.*)

MILLIE

I gotta lead! I gotta lead.

> (ROSEMARY *and* MILLIE *dance together in a trim, automatic way that keeps time to the music but little else. Both women seem to show a little arrogance in dancing together, as though boasting to the men of their independence. Their rhythm is accurate but uninspired.* HOWARD *and* HAL *watch, laughing.*)

HOWARD

S'posin' Hal and I did that.

ROSEMARY

Go ahead for all I care. (HOWARD *turns to* HAL *and, laughing, they start dancing together,* HAL *giving his own version of a coy female.* ROSEMARY *is irritated by this*) Stop it!

HOWARD

I thought we were doin' very nicely.

> (ROSEMARY *grabs* HOWARD *and pulls him up on the porch.*)

HAL

Come and dance with me, Millie!

MILLIE

Well—I never danced with boys. I always have to lead.

HAL

Just relax and do the steps I do. Come on and try.

(*They dance together but* MILLIE *has an awkward feeling of uncertainty that shows in her dancing.* HOWARD, *dancing with* ROSEMARY, *has been cutting up.*)

ROSEMARY

Quit clowning, Howard, and dance with me.

HOWARD

Honey, you don't get any fun out of dancing with *me*.

ROSEMARY

The band's playin'. You gotta dance with *some*one.

(*They resume an uncertain toddle.*)

MILLIE
(*To* HAL)

Am I too bad?

HAL

Naw! You just need a little practice.

ROSEMARY
(*While dancing*)

Lord, I love to dance. At school, kids all called me the Dancin' Fool. Went somewhere dancin' every night!

MRS. POTTS
(*Coming out of kitchen, she sits and watches the dancers.* FLO *and* ALAN *appear and stand in doorway watching*)

I can't stay in the kitchen while there's dancing!

HAL

(*Stops the dancing to deliver the needed instructions*)
Now look, kid, you gotta remember *I'm* the *man*, and you gotta do the steps *I* do.

MILLIE

I keep wantin' to do the steps I make up myself.

HAL

The man's gotta take the lead, kid, as long as he's able.

(*They resume dancing.*)

MRS. POTTS

You're doing fine, Millie!

MILLIE

(*As she is whirled around*)
I feel like Rita Hayworth!

(FLO *and* ALAN *go into the house.*)

ROSEMARY

(*Her youth returns in reverie*)
One night I went dancin' at a big Valentine party. I danced so hard I swooned! That's when they called me the Dancin' Fool.

HAL

(*Stops dancing for a moment*)
I'll show you a new step, kid. I learned this in L. A. Try it.

(*He nimbly executes a somewhat more intricate step.*)

MRS. POTTS

Isn't he graceful?

MILLIE

Gee, that looks hard.

HAL

Takes a little time. Give it a try!

(MILLIE *tries to do it, but it is too much for her.*)

MILLIE
(*Giving up*)

I'm sorry, I just can't seem to get it.

HAL

Watch close, kid. If you learn this step you'll be the sharp-
est kid in town. See?

(*He continues his demonstration.*)

MILLIE
(*Observing but baffled*)

Yah—but . . .

HAL

Real loose, see? You give it a little of this—and give it
a little of that.

(*He snaps his fingers, keeping a nimble, sensitive re-
sponse to the rhythm.*)

MILLIE

Gee, I wish *I* could do that.

(*Now the music changes to a slower, more sensuous
rhythm.* HAL *and* MILLIE *stop dancing and listen.*)

ROSEMARY
(*Who has been watching* HAL *enviously*)

That's the way to dance, Howard! That's the way.

(HAL *begins to dance to the slower rhythm and* MIL-
LIE *tries to follow him. Now* MADGE *comes out the
front door, wearing her new dress. Although the dress
is indeed "too fussy" for a picnic, she is ravishing.
She stands watching* HAL *and* MILLIE.)

HOWARD
(*Drifting from* ROSEMARY)
You sure look pretty, Madge.

MADGE
Thank you, Howard.

HOWARD
Would you like a little dance?

(*She accepts, and they dance together on the porch.*
ROSEMARY *is dancing by herself on the porch, upstage, and does not notice them.*)

MRS. POTTS
(*Seeing* MADGE *and* HOWARD *dancing*)
More dancers! We've turned the backyard into a ballroom!

ROSEMARY
(*Snatching* HOWARD *from* MADGE)
Thought you couldn't dance.

(MADGE *goes down into the yard and watches* HAL
and MILLIE.)

MRS. POTTS
(*To* MADGE)
The young man is teaching Millie a new step.

MADGE

Oh, that's fun. I've been trying to teach it to Alan.

(*She tries the step herself and does it as well as* HAL.)

MRS. POTTS

Look, everyone! Madge does it, too!

HAL
(*Turns around and sees* MADGE *dancing*)

Hey!

(*Some distance apart, snapping their fingers to the rhythm, their bodies respond without touching. Then they dance slowly toward each other and* HAL *takes her in his arms. The dance has something of the nature of a primitive rite that would mate the two young people. The others watch rather solemnly.*)

MRS. POTTS
(*Finally*)

It's like they were *made* to dance together, isn't it?

(*This remark breaks the spell.* MILLIE *moves to* MRS. POTTS' *steps and sits quietly in the background, beginning to inspect the bottle of whiskey.*)

ROSEMARY
(*Impatiently to* HOWARD)

Can't *you* dance that way?

HOWARD

Golly, Honey, I'm a businessman.

ROSEMARY
(*Dances by herself, kicking her legs in the air.* MIL-
LIE *takes an occasional drink from the whiskey bottle
during the following scene, unobserved by the others*)
I danced so hard one night, I swooned! Right in the center
of the ballroom!

HOWARD
(*Amused and observing*)
Rosemary's got pretty legs, hasn't she?

ROSEMARY
(*This strikes her as hilarious*)
That's just like you men, can't talk about anything but
women's legs.

HOWARD
(*A little offended to be misinterpreted*)
I just noticed they had a nice shape.

ROSEMARY
(*Laughing uproariously*)
How would you like it if we women went around talkin'
'bout *your* legs all the time?

HOWARD
(*Ready to be a sport, stands and lifts his trousers to
his knees*)
All right! There's *my* legs if you wanta talk about them.

ROSEMARY
(*She explodes with laughter*)
Never saw anything so ugly. Men's big hairy legs! (ROSE-
MARY *goes over to* HAL, *yanking him from* MADGE *posses-
sively*) Young man, let's see your legs.

HAL

(*Not knowing what to make of his seizure*)

Huh?

ROSEMARY

We passed a new rule here tonight. Every man here's gotta show his legs.

HAL

Mam, I got on boots.

HOWARD

Let the young man alone, Rosemary. He's dancin' with Madge.

ROSEMARY

Now it's his turn to dance with *me*. (*To* HAL) I may be an old-maid schoolteacher, but *I* can keep up with you. Ride 'em cowboy!

(*A little tight, stimulated by* HAL's *physical presence, she abandons convention and grabs* HAL *closely to her, plastering a cheek next to his and holding her hips fast against him. One can sense that* HAL *is embarrassed and repelled.*)

HAL

(*Wanting to object*)

Mam, I . . .

ROSEMARY

I used to have a boy friend was a cowboy. Met him in Colorado when I went out there to get over a case of flu. He was in love with me, 'cause I was an older woman and had some sense. Took me up in the mountains one night and made love. Wanted me to marry him right there on the mountain top. Said God'd be our preacher, the moon our best man. Ever hear such talk?

HAL
(*Trying to get away*)
Mam, I'd like another li'l drink now.

ROSEMARY
(*Jerking him closer to her*)
Dance with me, young man. Dance with me. I can keep up
with you. You know what? You remind me of one of those
ancient statues. There was one in the school library until last
year. He was a Roman gladiator. All he had on was a shield.
(*She gives a bawdy laugh*) A shield over his arm. That was
all he had on. All we girls felt insulted, havin' to walk past
that statue every time we went to the library. We got up a
petition and made the principal do something about it. (*She
laughs hilariously during her narration*) You know what he
did? He got the school janitor to fix things right. He got a
chisel and made that statue decent. (*Another bawdy laugh*)
Lord, those ancient people were depraved.

HAL
(*He seldom has been made so uncomfortable*)
Mam, I guess I just don't feel like dancin'.

ROSEMARY
(*Sobering from her story, grabs for* HAL, *catching
him by the shirt*)
Where you goin'?

HAL
Mam, I . . .

ROSEMARY
(*Commanding him imploringly*)
Dance with me, young man. Dance with me.

HAL

I . . . I . . .

(*He pulls loose from her grasp but her hand, still clutching, tears off a strip of his shirt as he gets away.* HOWARD *intervenes.*)

HOWARD

He wants to dance with Madge, Rosemary. Let 'em alone. They're young people.

ROSEMARY
(*In a hollow voice*)

Young? What do you mean, they're *young*?

MILLIE
(*A sick groan from the background*)

Oh, I'm sick.

MRS. POTTS

Millie!

MILLIE

I wanna die.

(*All eyes are on* MILLIE *now as she runs over to the kitchen door.*)

MADGE

Millie!

HOWARD

What'd the little Dickens do? Get herself tight?

HAL

Take it easy, kid.

ROSEMARY

(*She has problems of her own. She gropes blindly across the stage, suffering what has been a deep humiliation*)

I suppose that's something wonderful—they're *young*.

MADGE

(*Going to* MILLIE)

Let's go inside, Millie.

MILLIE

(*Turning on* MADGE *viciously*)

I *hate* you!

MADGE

(*Hurt*)

Millie!

MILLIE

(*Sobbing*)

Madge is the pretty one—Madge is the pretty one.

(MILLIE *dashes inside the kitchen door,* MRS. POTTS *behind her.*)

MADGE

(*To herself*)

What did she have to do that for?

HOWARD

(*Examining the bottle*)

She must have had several good snifters.

ROSEMARY

(*Pointing a finger at* HAL. *She has found vengeance*)

It's all *his* fault, Howard.

HOWARD

Now, Honey . . .

ROSEMARY
(*To* HAL, *defiantly and accusingly*)
Millie was your date. You shoulda been looking after her.
But you were too busy making eyes at Madge.

HOWARD

Honey . . .

ROSEMARY

And you're no better than he is, Madge. You should be
ashamed.

FLO
(*Flies out on the porch in a fury*)
Who fed whiskey to my Millie?

ROSEMARY
(*Pointing fanatically at* HAL)
He did, Mrs. Owens! It's all his fault!

(FLO *glares at* HAL.)

HOWARD
(*Trying to straighten things out*)
Mrs. Owens, it was this way . . .

FLO
My Millie is too young to be drinking whiskey!

ROSEMARY
Oh, he'd have fed her whiskey and taken his pleasure with
the child and then skidaddled!

HOWARD
(*Trying to bring them to reason*)
Now listen, everyone. Let's . . .

ROSEMARY
I know what I'm doing, Howard! And I don't need any
advice from *you*. (*Back at* HAL) You been stomping around
here in those boots like you owned the place, thinking every
woman you saw was gonna fall madly in love. But here's one
woman didn't pay you any mind.

HOWARD
The boy hasn't done anything, Mrs. Owens!

ROSEMARY
(*Facing* HAL, *drawing closer with each accusation*)
Aristocratic millionaire, my foot! You wouldn't know an
aristocratic millionaire if he spit on you. Braggin' about your
father, and I bet he wasn't any better'n you are.

> (HAL *is as though paralyzed.* HOWARD *still tries to
> reason with* FLO.)

HOWARD
None of us saw Millie drink the whiskey.

ROSEMARY
(*Closer to* HAL)
You think just cause you're a man, you can walk in here
and make off with whatever you like. You think just cause
you're young you can push other people aside and not pay
them any mind. You think just cause you're strong you can
show your muscles and nobody'll know what a pitiful speci-
men you are. But you won't stay young forever, didja ever

thinka that? What'll become of you then? You'll end your
life in the gutter and it'll serve you right, 'cause the gutter's
where you came from and the gutter's where you belong.

(*She has thrust her face into* HAL's *and is spitting
her final words at him before* HOWARD *finally grabs
her, almost as though to protect her from herself, and
holds her arms at her sides, pulling her away.*)

HOWARD

Rosemary, shut your damn mouth.

(HAL *withdraws to the far edge of the porch, no one
paying any attention to him now, his reaction to the
attack still a mystery.*)

MRS. POTTS
(*Comes out of kitchen*)

Millie's going to be perfectly all right, Flo. Alan held her
head and let her be sick. She's going to be perfectly all right
now.

FLO
(*A general announcement, clear and firm*)

I want it understood by everyone that there's to be no
more drinking on this picnic.

HOWARD

It was all my fault, Mrs. Owens. My fault.

(ALAN *escorts a sober* MILLIE *out on the porch.*)

MRS. POTTS

Here's Millie now, good as new. And we're all going on
the picnic and forget it.

ALAN
(*Quick to accuse* HAL)
Hal, what's happened?

(HAL *does not respond.*)

FLO
(*To* ALAN)
Millie will come with *us*, Alan.

ALAN
Sure, Mrs. Owens. Hal, I told you not to drink!

(HAL *is still silent.*)

FLO
Madge, why did you wear your new dress?

MADGE
(*As though mystified at herself*)
I don't know. I just put it on.

FLO
Go upstairs and change, this minute. I mean it! You come
later with Rosemary and Howard!

(MADGE *runs inside.*)

MRS. POTTS
Let's hurry. All the tables will be taken.

ALAN
Mr. Bevans, tell Madge I'll see her out there. Hal, the baskets are all in the Ford. Get goin'.

(HAL *doesn't move.* ALAN *hurries off.*)

FLO

Millie, darling, are you feeling better?

(FLO *and* MILLIE *go off through alley, right.*)

MRS. POTTS

(*To* HAL)

Young man, you can follow us and find the way.

(MRS. POTTS *follows the others off. We hear the Cadillac drive off.* HAL *is sitting silent and beaten on the edge of the porch.* HOWARD *and* ROSEMARY *are on the lawn by* MRS. POTTS' *house.*)

HOWARD

He's just a boy, Rosemary. You talked awful.

ROSEMARY

What made me do it, Howard? What made me act that way?

HOWARD

You gotta remember, men have got feelings, too—same as women. (*To* HAL) Don't pay any attention to her, young man. She didn't mean a thing.

ROSEMARY

(*Has gone up to the gate*)

I don't want to go on the picnic, Howard. This is my last night of vacation and I want to have a good time.

HOWARD

We'll go for a ride, Honey.

ROSEMARY

I want to drive into the sunset, Howard! I want to drive
into the sunset!

(*She runs off toward the car,* HOWARD *following.*
HOWARD's *car drives away.* HAL *sits on the porch,
defeated.* MADGE *soon comes out in another dress.
She comes out very quietly and he makes no recog-
nition of her presence. She sits on a bench on the
porch and finally speaks in a soft voice.*)

MADGE

You're a wonderful dancer . . .

HAL
(*Hardly audible*)

Thanks.

MADGE

. . . and I can tell a lot about a boy by dancing with him.
Some boys, even though they're very smart, or very successful
in some other way, when they take a girl in their arms to
dance, they're sort of awkward and a girl feels sort of uncomfortable.

HAL
(*He keeps his head down, his face in his hands*)

Yah.

MADGE

But when you took me in your arms—to dance—I had the
most relaxed feeling, that you knew what you were doing, and
I could follow every step of the way.

HAL

Look, Baby, I'm in a pretty bad mood.

(*He stands suddenly and walks away from her, his
hands thrust into his pockets. He is uncomfortable to
be near her, for he is trembling with insult and rage.*)

MADGE

You mustn't pay any attention to Miss Sydney. (HAL *is
silent*) Women like her make me mad at the whole female
sex.

HAL

Look, Baby, why don't you beat it?

MADGE

(*She is aware of the depth of his feelings*)
What's the matter?

HAL

(*Gives up and begins to shudder, his shoulders heav-
ing as he fights to keep from bawling*)
What's the use, Baby? I'm a bum. She saw through me
like a God-damn X-ray machine. There's just no place in the
world for a guy like me.

MADGE

There's got to be.

HAL

(*With self-derision*)
Yah?

MADGE

Of course. You're young, and—you're very entertaining. I
mean—you say all sorts of witty things, and I just loved listening to you talk. And you're strong and—you're very good-
looking. I bet Miss Sydney thought so, too, or she wouldn't
have said those things.

HAL

Look, Baby, lemme level with you. When I was fourteen, I spent a year in the reform school. How ya like that?

MADGE

Honest?

HAL

Yah!

MADGE

What for?

HAL

For stealin' another guy's motorcycle. Yah! I *stole* it. I stole it 'cause I wanted to get on the damn thing and go so far away, so fast, that no one'd ever catch up with me.

MADGE

I think—lots of boys feel that way at times.

HAL

Then my old lady went to the authorities. (*He mimics his "old lady"*) "I've done everything I can with the boy. I can't do anything more." So off I go to the God-damn reform school.

MADGE
(*With all the feeling she has*)

Gee!

HAL

Finally some welfare league hauls me out and the old lady's sorry to see me back. Yah! she's got herself a new boy friend and I'm in the way.

MADGE

It's awful when parents don't get along.

HAL

I never told that to another soul, not even Seymour.

MADGE

(*At a loss*)

I—I wish there was something I could say—or *do*.

HAL

Well—that's the Hal Carter story, but no one's ever gonna make a movie of it.

MADGE

(*To herself*)

Most people would be awfully shocked.

HAL

(*Looking at her, then turning away cynically*)

There you are, Baby. If you wanta faint—or get sick—or run in the house and lock the doors—go ahead. I aint stoppin' you. (*There is a silence. Then* MADGE, *suddenly and impulsively, takes his face in her hands and kisses him. Then she returns her hands to her lap and feels embarrassed.* HAL *looks at her in amazement*) Baby! What'd you do?

MADGE

I . . . I'm proud you told me.

HAL

(*With humble appreciation*)

Baby!

MADGE

I . . . I get so tired of being told I'm pretty.

HAL

(*Folding her in his arms caressingly*)
Baby, Baby, Baby.

MADGE

(*Resisting him, jumping to her feet*)
Don't. We have to go. We have all the baskets in our car
and they'll be waiting. (HAL *gets up and walks slowly to
her, their eyes fastened and* MADGE *feeling a little thrill of
excitement as he draws nearer*) Really—we have to be going.
(HAL *takes her in his arms and kisses her passionately. Then*
MADGE *utters his name in a voice of resignation*) Hal!

HAL

Just be quiet, Baby.

MADGE

Really . . . We have to go. They'll be waiting.

HAL

(*Picking her up in his arms and starting off. His
voice is deep and firm*)
We're not goin' on no God-damn picnic.

CURTAIN

ACT THREE

ACT THREE

SCENE I

*It is after midnight. A great harvest moon shines in the
sky, a deep, murky blue. The moon is swollen and full
and casts a pale light on the scene below. Soon we hear*
HOWARD's *Chevrolet chugging to a stop by the house, then*
HOWARD *and* ROSEMARY *come on,* ROSEMARY *first. Wearily,
a groggy depression having set in, she makes her way to the
doorstep and drops there, sitting limp. She seems preoccupied
at first and her responses to* HOWARD *are mere grunts.*

HOWARD

Here we are, Honey. Right back where we started from.

ROSEMARY
(*Her mind elsewhere*)

Uhh.

HOWARD

You were awful nice to me tonight, Rosemary.

ROSEMARY

Uhh.

HOWARD

Do you think Mrs. Owens suspects anything?

ROSEMARY

I don't care if she does.

123

HOWARD

A businessman's gotta be careful of talk. And after all, you're a schoolteacher. (*Fumbling to get away*) Well, I better be gettin' back to Cherryvale. I gotta open up the store in the morning. Good night, Rosemary.

ROSEMARY

Uhh.

HOWARD
(*He pecks at her cheek with a kiss*)
Good night. Maybe I should say, good morning.

(*He starts off.*)

ROSEMARY
(*Just coming to*)
Where you goin', Howard?

HOWARD

Honey, I gotta get home.

ROSEMARY

You can't go off without me.

HOWARD

Honey, talk sense.

ROSEMARY

You can't go off without me. Not after tonight. *That's* sense.

HOWARD
(*A little nervous*)
Honey, be reasonable.

ROSEMARY

Take me with you.

HOWARD

What'd people say?

ROSEMARY
(*Almost vicious*)
To *hell* with what people'd say!

HOWARD
(*Shocked*)

Honey!

ROSEMARY

What'd people say if I thumbed my nose at them? What'd people say if I walked down the street and showed 'em my pink panties? What do I care what people say?

HOWARD

Honey, you're not yourself tonight.

ROSEMARY

Yes, I am. I'm more myself than I ever was. Take me with you, Howard. If you don't I don't know what I'll do with myself. I mean it.

HOWARD

Now look, Honey, you better go upstairs and get some sleep. You gotta start school in the morning. We'll talk all this over Saturday.

ROSEMARY

Maybe you won't be back Saturday. Maybe you won't be back ever again.

HOWARD

Rosemary, you know better than that.

ROSEMARY

Then what's the next thing in store for me? To be nice
to the next man, then the next—till there's no one left to
care whether I'm nice to him or not. Till I'm ready for the
grave and don't have anyone to take me there.

HOWARD
(*In an attempt to be consoling*)

Now, Rosemary!

ROSEMARY

You can't let that happen to me, Howard. I won't let you.

HOWARD

I don't understand. When we first started going together,
you were the best sport I ever saw, always good for a laugh.

ROSEMARY
(*In a hollow voice*)

I can't laugh any more.

HOWARD

We'll talk it over Saturday.

ROSEMARY

We'll talk it over *now*.

HOWARD
(*Squirming*)

Well—Honey—I . . .

ROSEMARY

You said you were gonna marry me, Howard. You said
when I got back from my vacation, you'd be waitin' with the
preacher.

HOWARD

Honey, I've had an awful busy summer and . . .

ROSEMARY

Where's the preacher, Howard? Where is he?

HOWARD

(*Walking away from her*)

Honey, I'm forty-two years old. A person forms certain
ways of livin', then one day it's too late to change.

ROSEMARY

(*Grabbing his arm and holding him*)

Come back here, Howard. I'm no spring chicken either.
Maybe I'm a little older than you think *I* am. I've formed
my ways too. But they can be changed. They *gotta* be changed.
It's no good livin' like this, in rented rooms, meetin' a bunch
of old maids for supper every night, then comin' back home
alone.

HOWARD

I know how it is, Rosemary. My life's no bed of roses
either.

ROSEMARY

Then why don't you do something about it?

HOWARD

I figure—there's some bad things about every life.

ROSEMARY

There's too much bad about mine. Each year, I keep tellin'
myself, is the last. Something'll happen. Then nothing ever
does—except I get a little crazier all the time.

HOWARD
(*Hopelessly*)
Well . . .

ROSEMARY

A *well's* a hole in the ground, Howard. Be careful you
don't fall in.

HOWARD

I wasn't tryin' to be funny.

ROSEMARY

. . . and all this time you just been leadin' me on.

HOWARD
(*Defensive*)
Rosemary, that's not *so*! I've not been leading you *on*.

ROSEMARY

I'd like to know what else you call it.

HOWARD

Well—can't we talk about it Saturday? I'm dead tired and
I got a busy week ahead, and . . .

ROSEMARY
(*She grips him by the arm and looks straight into
his eyes*)
You gotta marry me, Howard.

HOWARD
(*Tortured*)
Well—Honey, I can't marry you *now*.

ROSEMARY
You can be over here in the morning.

HOWARD
Sometimes you're unreasonable.

ROSEMARY
You gotta marry me.

HOWARD
What'll you do about your job?

ROSEMARY
Alvah Jackson can take my place till they get someone
new from the agency.

HOWARD
I'll have to pay Fred Jenkins to take care of the store for
a few days.

ROSEMARY
Then get him.

HOWARD
Well . . .

ROSEMARY
I'll be waitin' for you in the morning, Howard.

HOWARD
(*After a few moments' troubled thought*)
No.

ROSEMARY
(*A muffled cry*)
Howard!

HOWARD
I'm not gonna marry anyone that says, "You gotta marry me, Howard." I'm not gonna. (*He is silent.* ROSEMARY *weeps pathetic tears. Slowly* HOWARD *reconsiders*) If a woman wants me to marry her—she can at least say "please."

ROSEMARY
(*Beaten and humble*)
Please marry me, Howard.

HOWARD
Well—you got to give me time to think it over.

ROSEMARY
(*Desperate*)
Oh, God! Please marry me, Howard. Please . . . (*She sinks to her knees*) Please . . . please . . .

HOWARD
(*Embarrassed by her suffering humility*)
Rosemary . . . I . . . I gotta have some time to think it over. You go to bed now and get some rest. I'll drive over in the morning and maybe we can talk it over before you go to school. I . . .

ROSEMARY

You're not just tryin' to get out of it, Howard?

HOWARD

I'll be over in the morning, Honey.

ROSEMARY

Honest?

HOWARD

Yah. I gotta go to the courthouse anyway. We'll talk it over then.

ROSEMARY

Oh, God, please marry me, Howard. Please.

HOWARD

(*Trying to get away*)

Go to bed, Honey. I'll see you in the morning.

ROSEMARY

Please, Howard!

HOWARD

I'll see you in the morning. Good night, Rosemary.

(*Starting off.*)

ROSEMARY

(*In a meek voice*)

Please!

HOWARD

Good night, Rosemary.

ROSEMARY
(*After he is gone*)

Please.

> (ROSEMARY *stands alone on the doorstep. We hear
> the sound of* HOWARD's *car start up and drive off,
> chugging away in the distance.* ROSEMARY *is drained
> of energy. She pulls herself together and goes into
> the house. The stage is empty for several moments.
> Then* MADGE *runs on from the back, right. Her face
> is in her hands. She is sobbing.* HAL *follows fast be-
> hind. He reaches her just as she gets to the door, and
> grabs her by the wrist. She resists him furiously.*)

HAL

Baby . . . you're not sorry, are you?
(*There is a silence.* MADGE *sobs.*)

MADGE

Let me go.

HAL

Please, Baby. If I thought I'd done anything to make you
unhappy, I . . . I'd almost wanta die.

MADGE

I . . . I'm so ashamed.

HAL

Don't say that, Baby.

MADGE

I didn't even know what was happening, and then . . . all
of a sudden, it seems like my whole life was changed.

HAL
(*With bitter self-disparagement*)

I oughta be taken out and hung. I'm just a no-good bum.
That schoolteacher was right. I oughta be in the gutter.

MADGE

Don't talk that way.

HAL

Times like this, I hate myself, Baby.

MADGE

I guess . . . it's no more your fault than mine.

HAL

Sometimes I do pretty impulsive things. (MADGE *starts inside*) Will I see you tomorrow?

MADGE

I don't know.

HAL

Gee, I almost forgot. I start a new job tomorrow.

MADGE

I have to be at the dime store at nine.

HAL

What time you through?

MADGE

Five.

HAL

Maybe I could see you then, huh? Maybe I could come by and . . .

MADGE

I've got a date with Alan—if he'll still speak to me.

HAL
(*A new pain*)
Jesus, I'd forgot all about Seymour.

MADGE

So had I.

HAL

I can't go back to his house. What'll I do?

MADGE

Maybe Mrs. Potts could . . .

HAL

I'll take the car back to where we were, stretch out in the front seat and get a little sleep. (*He thinks a moment*) Baby, how you gonna handle your old lady?

MADGE
(*With a slight tremor*)
I . . . I don't know.

HAL
(*In a funk again*)
Jesus, I oughta be shot at sunrise.

MADGE
I . . . I'll think of something to tell her.

HAL
(*Awkward*)
Well—good night.

MADGE
Good night.
(*She starts again.*)

HAL
Baby—would you kiss me good night . . . maybe? Just one
more time.

MADGE
I don't think I better.

HAL
Please!

MADGE
It . . . It'd just start things all over again. Things I better
forget.

HAL
Pretty please!

MADGE
Promise not to hold me?

HAL

I'll keep my hands to my side. Swear to God!

MADGE

Well . . .

(*Slowly she goes toward him, takes his face in her hands and kisses him. The kiss lasts.* HAL's *hands become nervous and finally find their way around her. Their passion is revived. Then* MADGE *utters a little shriek, tears herself away from* HAL *and runs into the house, sobbing.*)

Don't. You *promised*. I never wanta see you again. I might as well be dead.

(*She runs inside the front door, leaving* HAL *behind to despise himself. He beats his fists together, kicks the earth with his heel, and starts off, hating the day he was born.*)

CURTAIN

ACT THREE

Scene II

It is very early the next morning. MILLIE *sits on the door-step smoking a cigarette. She wears a fresh wash dress in honor of the first day of school.* FLO *breaks out of the front door. She is a frantic woman.* MILLIE *puts out her cigarette quickly.* FLO *has not even taken the time to dress. She wears an old robe over her nightdress. She speaks to* MILLIE.

FLO

Were you awake when Madge got in?

MILLIE

No.

FLO

Did she say anything to you this morning?

MILLIE

No.

FLO

Dear God! I couldn't get two words out of her last night, she was crying so hard. Now she's got the door locked.

MILLIE

I bet I know what happened.

137

FLO
(Sharply)

You don't know anything, Millie Owens. And if anyone says anything to you, you just . . . (*Now she sniffs the air*) Have you been smoking?

MRS. POTTS
(Coming down her backsteps)

Did Madge tell you what happened?

FLO

The next time you take in tramps, Helen Potts, I'll thank you to keep them on your own side of the yard.

MRS. POTTS

Is Madge all right?

FLO

Of course she's all right. She got out of the car and left that hoodlum alone. That's what she did.

MRS. POTTS

Have you heard from Alan?

FLO

He said he'd be over this morning.

MRS. POTTS

Where's the young man?

FLO

I know where he should be! He should be in the penitentiary, and that's where he's going if he shows up around here again!

ROSEMARY

(*Sticking her head out front door*)

Has anyone seen Howard?

FLO

(*Surprised*)

Howard? Why, no, Rosemary!

ROSEMARY

(*Nervous and uncertain*)

He said he might be over this morning. Mrs. Owens, I'm storing my summer clothes in the attic. Could someone help me?

FLO

We're busy, Rosemary.

MRS. POTTS

I'll help you, Rosemary.

(*She looks at* FLO, *then goes up on porch.*)

ROSEMARY

Thanks, Mrs. Potts.

(*Goes inside.*)

FLO

(*To* MRS. POTTS)

She's been running around like a chicken with its head off all morning. Something's *up*! (MRS. POTTS *goes inside.* FLO *turns to* MILLIE) You keep watch for Alan.

(FLO *goes inside. Now we hear the morning voices of* IRMA *and* CHRISTINE, *coming by for* ROSEMARY.)

IRMA

Girl, I hope Rosemary is ready. I promised the principal that I'd be there early to help with registration.

CHRISTINE

How do I look, Irma?

IRMA

It's a cute dress. Let me fix it in the back.

(IRMA *adjusts the hang of the dress as* CHRISTINE *stands patiently.*)

CHRISTINE

I think a teacher should dress up first day of school, to give the students a good first impression.

IRMA

(*Going up on the porch*)

Good morning, Millie!

MILLIE

Hi.

IRMA

Is Rosemary ready?

MILLIE

Go on up if you want to.

CHRISTINE

(*To* MILLIE)

We missed seeing Madge on the picnic last night.

MILLIE

So did a lot of other people.

IRMA

(*Gives* CHRISTINE *a significant look*)

Come on, Christine. I bet we have to get that sleepy girl out of bed.

(*They go inside front door.* BOMBER *rides on, gets off his bicycle, throws a paper on* MRS. POTTS' *steps, then on* FLO's *back porch. Then he climbs up on* MRS. POTTS' *porch so he can look across into* MADGE's *room*)

BOMBER

Hey, Madge! Wanta go dancin'? Let me be next, Madge!

MILLIE

You shut up, Crazy.

BOMBER

My brother seen 'em parked under the bridge. Alan Seymour was lookin' for 'em all over town. She always put on a lot of airs, but I knew she liked guys.

(*He sees* ALAN *approaching from beyond the* OWENS' *house, and leaves quickly.*)

MILLIE

Some day I'm really gonna kill that ornery bastard.

(*She turns and sees* ALAN.)

ALAN

Could I see Madge?

MILLIE

I'll call her, Alan. (*Calls up to* MADGE's *window*) Madge! Alan's here! (*Back to* ALAN) She prob'ly has to dress.

ALAN

I'll wait.

MILLIE

(*She sits on the stump and turns to him very shyly*)
I . . . I always liked you, Alan. Didn't you know it?

ALAN

(*With some surprise*)
Like me?

MILLIE

(*Nods her head*)
It's awfully hard to show someone you like them, isn't it?

ALAN

(*With just a little bitterness*)
It's easy for *some* people.

MILLIE

It makes you feel like such a sap. I don't know why.

ALAN

(*Rather touched*)
I . . . I'm glad you like me, Millie.

MILLIE

(*One can sense her loneliness*)
I don't expect you to do anything about it. I just wanted
to tell you.

(HOWARD *comes bustling on through the gate, very
upset. He addresses* MILLIE.)

HOWARD

Could I see Rosemary?

MILLIE

My gosh, Howard, what are you doing here?

HOWARD

I think she's expecting me.

MILLIE

You better holler at the bottom of the stairs—(HOWARD
is about to go in the door, but turns back at this) all the
others are up there, too.

HOWARD
(*He looks very grave*)

The others?

MILLIE

Mrs. Potts and Miss Kronkite and Miss Schoenwalder.

HOWARD

Golly, I gotta see her alone.

ROSEMARY
(*Calling from inside*)

Howard! (*Inside, to all the women*) It's Howard! He's
here!

HOWARD
(*Knowing he is stuck*)

Golly!

(*We hear a joyful babble of women's voices from
inside.* HOWARD *gives one last pitiful look at* MILLIE,
then goes in. MILLIE *follows him in and* ALAN *is left*

alone in the yard. After a moment, MADGE *comes out the kitchen door. She wears a simple dress, and her whole being appears chastened. She is inscrutable in her expression.*)

MADGE

Hello, Alan.

ALAN

(*Very moved by seeing her*)

Madge!

MADGE

I'm sorry about last night.

ALAN

Madge, whatever happened—it wasn't your fault. I know what Hal's like when he's drinking. But I've got Hal taken care of now! He won't be bothering you again!

MADGE

Honest?

ALAN

At school I spent half of my life getting him out of jams. I knew he'd had a few tough breaks, and I always tried to be sorry for the guy. But this is the thanks I get.

MADGE

(*Still noncommittal*)

Where is he now?

ALAN

Don't worry about Hal! I'll take it on myself now to offer you his official good-bye!

MADGE
(*One still cannot decipher her feelings*)
Is he gone?

FLO
(*Running out kitchen door. She is dressed now*)
Alan, I didn't know you were here!

(*Now we hear shouts from inside the house.* MILLIE
*comes out, throwing rice over her shoulder at all the
the others, who are laughing and shouting so that we
only hear bits of the following.*)

MRS. POTTS
Here comes the bride! Here comes the bride!

IRMA
May all your troubles be little ones!

CHRISTINE
You're getting a wonderful girl, Howard Bevans!

IRMA
Rosemary is getting a fine man!

CHRISTINE
They don't come any better'n Rosemary!

MRS. POTTS
Be happy!

IRMA
May all your troubles be little ones!

MRS. POTTS

Be happy forever and ever!

> (*Now they are all out on the porch and we see that* HOWARD *carries two suitcases. His face has an expression of complete confusion.* ROSEMARY *wears a fussy going-away outfit.*)

IRMA

(*To* ROSEMARY)

Girl, are you wearing something old?

ROSEMARY

An old pair of nylons but they're as good as new.

CHRISTINE

And that's a brand-new outfit she's got on. Rosemary, are you wearing something blue? I don't see it!

ROSEMARY

(*Daringly*)

And you're not gonna! (*They all laugh, and* ROSEMARY *begins a personal inventory*) Something borrowed! I don't have anything to borrow!

> (*Now we see* HAL's *head appear from the edge of the woodshed. He watches for a moment when he can be sure of not being observed, then darts into the shed.*)

FLO

Madge, you give Rosemary something to borrow. It'll mean good luck for you. Go on, Madge! (*She takes* ALAN's *arm and pulls him toward the steps with her*) Rosemary, Madge has something for you to borrow!

MADGE
(*Crossing to the group by steps*)
You can borrow my handkerchief, Miss Sydney.

ROSEMARY
Thank you, Madge. (*She takes the handkerchief*) Isn't
Madge pretty, girls?

IRMA AND CHRISTINE
Oh, yes! Yes, indeed!

(MADGE *turns and leaves the group, going toward*
MRS. POTTS' *house.*)

ROSEMARY
(*During the above*)
She's modest! A girl as pretty as Madge can sail through
life without a care!

(ALAN *turns from the group to join* MADGE. FLO
then turns and crosses toward MADGE. ROSEMARY *follows* FLO.)

Mrs. Owens, I left my hot-water bottle in the closet and
my curlers are in the bathroom. You and the girls can have
them. I stored the rest of my things in the attic. Howard and
I'll come and get 'em after we settle down. Cherryvale's not
so far away. We can be good friends, same as before.

(HAL *sticks his head through woodshed door and
catches* MADGE's *eye.* MADGE *is startled.*)

FLO
I hate to mention it now, Rosemary, but you didn't give
us much notice. Do you know anyone I could rent the room
to?

IRMA
(*To* ROSEMARY)
Didn't you tell her about Linda Sue Breckenridge?

ROSEMARY
Oh, yes! Linda Sue Breckenridge—she's the sewing teacher!

IRMA
(*A positive affirmation to them all*)
And she's a darling girl!

ROSEMARY
She and Mrs. Bendix had a fight. Mrs. Bendix wanted to charge her twenty cents for her orange juice in the morning and none of us girls ever paid more'n fifteen. Did we, girls?

IRMA AND CHRISTINE
(*In staunch support*)
No! Never! I certainly never did!

ROSEMARY
Irma, you tell Linda Sue to get in touch with Mrs. Owens.

IRMA
I'll do that very thing.

FLO
Thank you, Rosemary.

HOWARD
Rosemary, we still got to pick up the license . . .

ROSEMARY

(*To* IRMA *and* CHRISTINE, *all of them blubbering*)
Good-bye, girls! We've had some awfully jolly times together!

(IRMA, CHRISTINE *and* ROSEMARY *embrace*.)

HOWARD
(*A little restless*)

Come on, Honey!

(ALAN *takes the suitcases from* HOWARD.)

HOWARD
(*To* ALAN)

A man's gotta settle down some time.

ALAN

Of course.

HOWARD

And folks'd rather do business with a married man!

ROSEMARY
(*To* MADGE *and* ALAN)

I hope both of you are going to be as happy as Howard and I will be. (*Turns to* MRS. POTTS) You've been a wonderful friend, Mrs. Potts!

MRS. POTTS

I wish you all sorts of happiness, Rosemary.

ROSEMARY

Good-bye, Millie. You're going to be a famous author some day and I'll be proud I knew you.

MILLIE

Thanks, Miss Sydney.

HOWARD
(*To* ROSEMARY)

All set?

ROSEMARY

All set and rarin' to go! (*A sudden thought*) Where we goin'?

HOWARD
(*After an awkward pause*)

Well . . . I got a cousin who runs a tourist camp in the Ozarks. He and his wife could put us up for free.

ROSEMARY

Oh, I love the Ozarks!

(*She grabs* HOWARD's *arm and pulls him off stage.* ALAN *carries the suitcase off stage.* IRMA, CHRISTINE, MRS. POTTS *and* MILLIE *follow them, all throwing rice and calling after them.*)

ALL
(*As they go off*)

The Ozarks are lovely this time of year!
Be happy!
May all your troubles be little ones!
You're getting a wonderful girl!
You're getting a wonderful man!

FLO
(*Alone with* MADGE)

Madge, what happened last night? You haven't told me a word.

MADGE

Let me alone, Mom.

ROSEMARY
(*Off stage*)

Mrs. Owens, aren't you going to tell us good-bye?

FLO
(*Exasperated*)
Oh, dear! I've been saying good-bye to her all morning.

ALAN
(*Appearing in gateway*)
Mrs. Owens, Miss Sydney wants to give you her house keys.

MRS. POTTS
(*Behind* ALAN)
Come on, Flo!

FLO
(*Hurrying off*)
I'm coming. I'm coming.

(*She follows* ALAN *and* MRS. POTTS *to join the noisy
shivaree in the background. Now* HAL *appears from
the woodshed. His clothes are drenched and cling
plastered to his body. He is barefoot and there is
blood on his T-shirt. He stands before* MADGE.)

HAL
Baby!

MADGE
(*Backing from him*)
You shouldn't have come here.

HAL
Look, Baby, I'm in a jam.

MADGE
Serves you right.

HAL

Seymour's old man put the cops on my tail. Accused me
of stealin' the car. I had to knock one of the bastards cold
and swim the river to get away. If they ever catch up with
me, it'll be too bad.

MADGE

(*Things are in a slightly different light now*)
You were born to get in trouble.

HAL

Baby, I just *had* to say good-bye.

MADGE

(*Still not giving away her feelings*)
Where you going?

HAL

The freight train's by pretty soon. I'll hop a ride. I done
it lotsa times before.

MADGE

What're you gonna do?

HAL

I got some friends in Tulsa. I can always get a job hoppin'
bells at the Hotel Mayo. Jesus, I hate to say good-bye.

MADGE

(*Not knowing what her precise feelings are*)
Well . . . I don't know what else there is to do.

HAL

Are you still mad, Baby?

MADGE
(*Evasively*)

I . . . I never knew a boy like you.

(*The shivaree is quieting down now, and* HOWARD
and ROSEMARY *can be heard driving off as the others
call.* FLO *returns, stopping in the gateway, seeing*
HAL.)

FLO

Madge!

(*Now* ALAN *comes running on.*)

ALAN
(*Incensed*)

Hal, what're you doing here?

(MRS. POTTS *and* MILLIE *come on, followed by* IRMA
and CHRISTINE.)

MRS. POTTS

It's the young man!

HAL

Look, Seymour, I didn't swipe your lousy car. Get that
straight!

ALAN

You better get out of town if you know what's good for
you.

HAL

I'll go when I'm ready.

MRS. POTTS

Go? I thought you were going to stay here and settle
down.

HAL
No'm. I'm not gonna settle down.

ALAN
(*Tearing into* HAL *savagely*)
You'll go *now*. What do you take me for?

HAL
(*Holding* ALAN *off, not wanting a fight*)
Look, Kid, I don't wanta fight with *you*. You're the only friend I ever had.

ALAN
We're not friends any more. I'm not scared of you.

(ALAN *plows into* HAL, *but* HAL *is far beyond him in strength and physical alertness. He fastens* ALAN's *arms quickly behind him and brings him to the ground.* IRMA *and* CHRISTINE *watch excitedly from the gateway.* MRS. POTTS *is apprehensive.* ALAN *cries out in pain*)

Let me go, you God-damn tramp! Let me go!

FLO
(*To* HAL)
Take your hands off him, this minute.

(*But* ALAN *has to admit he is mastered.* HAL *releases him and* ALAN *retires to* MRS. POTTS' *back doorstep, sitting there, holding his hands over his face, feeling the deepest humiliation. A train whistle is heard in the distance.* HAL *hurries to* MADGE's *side.*)

HAL
(*To* MADGE)
Baby, aren't you gonna say good-bye?

FLO

(*To* IRMA *and* CHRISTINE)

You better run along, girls. This is no side show we're running.

(*They depart in a huff.*)

MADGE

(*Keeping her head down, not wanting to look at* HAL)

. . . Good-bye . . .

HAL

Please don't be mad, Baby. You were sittin' there beside me lookin' so pretty, sayin' all those sweet things, and I . . . I thought you liked me, too, Baby. Honest I did.

MADGE

It's all right. I'm not mad.

HAL

Thanks. Thanks a lot.

FLO

(*Like a barking terrier*)

Young man, if you don't leave here this second, I'm going to call the police and have you put where you belong.

(MADGE *and* HAL *do not even hear.*)

MADGE

And I . . . I *did* like you . . . the first time I saw you.

FLO

(*Incensed*)

Madge!

HAL
(*Beaming*)
Honest? (MADGE *nods*) I kinda thought you did.

(*All has been worth it now for* HAL. MILLIE *watches skeptically from doorstep.* MRS. POTTS *looks on lovingly from the back.* FLO *at times concerns herself with* ALAN, *then with trying to get rid of* HAL.)

FLO
Madge, I want you inside the house this minute.
(MADGE *doesn't move.*)

HAL
Look, Baby, I never said it before. I never could. It made me feel like such a freak, but I . . .

MADGE
What?

HAL
I'm nuts about you, Baby. I mean it.

MADGE
You make love to lots of girls . . .

HAL
A few.

MADGE
. . . just like you made love to me last night.

HAL
Not like last night, Baby. Last night was . . . (*Gropes for the word*) *inspired.*

MADGE
Honest?

HAL

The way you sat there, knowin' just how I felt. The way
you held my hand and talked.

MADGE

I couldn't stand to hear Miss Sydney treat you that way.
After all, you're a man.

HAL

And you're a woman, Baby, whether you know it or not.
You're a real, live woman.

(*A police siren is heard stirring up the distance.* FLO,
MRS. POTTS *and* MILLIE *are alarmed.*)

MILLIE

Hey, it's the cops.

MRS. POTTS

I'll know how to take care of them.

(MRS. POTTS *hurries off, right,* MILLIE *watching.* HAL
and MADGE *have not moved. They stand looking into
each other's eyes. Then* HAL *speaks.*)

HAL

Do—do you love me?

MADGE

(*Tears forming in her eyes*)
What good is it if I do?

HAL

I'm a poor bastard, Baby. I've gotta claim the things in
this life that're mine. Kiss me good-bye. (*He grabs her and*

kisses her) Come with me, Baby. They gimme a room in the basement of the hotel. It's kinda crummy but we could share it till we found something better.

FLO
(*Outraged*)

Madge! Are you out of your senses?

MADGE

I couldn't.
(*The train whistles in the distance.*)

FLO

Young man, you'd better get on that train as fast as you can.

HAL
(*To* MADGE)

When you hear that train pull outa town and know I'm on it, your little heart's gonna be busted, cause you love me, God damn it! You love me, you love me, you love me.

(*He stamps one final kiss on her lips, then runs off to catch his train.* MADGE *falls in a heap when he releases her.* FLO *is quick to console* MADGE.)

FLO

Get up, girl.

MADGE

Oh, Mom!

FLO

Why did this have to happen to you?

MADGE

I *do* love him! I *do!*

FLO

Hush, girl. Hush. The neighbors are on their porches, watching.

MADGE

I never knew what the feeling was. Why didn't someone tell me?

MILLIE
(*Peering off at the back*)
He made it. He got on the train.

MADGE
(*A cry of deep regret*)
Now I'll never see him again.

FLO

Madge, believe me, that's for the best.

MADGE

Why? Why?

FLO

At least you didn't marry him.

MADGE
(*A wail of anguish*)
Oh, Mom, what can you do with the love you feel? Where is there you can take it?

FLO
(*Beaten and defeated*)
I . . . I never found out.

> (MADGE *goes into the house, crying.* MRS. POTTS *returns, carrying* HAL's *boots. She puts them on the porch.*)

MRS. POTTS
The police found these on the river bank.

ALAN
(*On* MRS. POTTS' *steps, rises*)
Girls have always liked Hal. Months after he'd left the fraternity, they still called. "Is Hal there?" "Does anyone know where Hal's gone?" Their voices always sounded so forlorn.

FLO
Alan, come to dinner tonight. I'm having sweet-potato pie and all the things you like.

ALAN
I'll be gone, Mrs. Owens.

FLO
Gone?

ALAN
Dad's been wanting me to take him up to Michigan on a fishing trip. I've been stalling him, but now I . . .

FLO
You'll be back before you go to school, won't you?

ALAN
I'll be back Christmas, Mrs. Owens.

FLO
Christmas! Alan, go inside and say good-bye to Madge!

ALAN
(*Recalling his past love*)
Madge is beautiful. It made me feel so proud—just to *look* at her—and tell myself she's mine.

FLO
See her one more time, Alan!

ALAN
(*His mind is made up*)
No! I'll be home Christmas. I'll run over then and—say hello.
(*He runs off.*)

FLO
(*A cry of loss*)
Alan!

MRS. POTTS
(*Consolingly*)
He'll be back, Flo. He'll be back.

MILLIE
(*Waving good-bye*)
Good-bye Alan!

FLO
(*Getting life started again*)
You better get ready for school, Millie.

MILLIE
(*Going to doorstep, rather sad*)
Gee, I almost forgot.
(*She goes inside. FLO turns to MRS. POTTS.*)

FLO

You—you liked the young man, didn't you, Helen? Admit it.

MRS. POTTS

Yes, I did.

FLO
(*Belittlingly*)

Hmm.

MRS. POTTS

With just Mama and me in the house, I'd got so used to things as they were, everything so prim, occasionally a hairpin on the floor, the geranium in the window, the smell of Mama's medicines . . .

FLO

I'll keep things as they are in *my* house, thank you.

MRS. POTTS

Not when a man is there, Flo. He walked through the door and suddenly everything was different. He clomped through the tiny rooms like he was still in the great outdoors, he talked in a booming voice that shook the ceiling. Everything he did reminded me there was a man in the house, and it seemed good.

FLO
(*Skeptically*)

Did it?

MRS. POTTS

And that reminded *me* . . . I'm a woman, and that seemed good, too.

(*Now* MILLIE *comes swaggering out the front door, carrying her schoolbooks.*)

MILLIE
(*Disparagingly*)
Madge is in love with that crazy guy. She's in there crying
her eyes out.

FLO
Mind your business and go to school.

MILLIE
I'm never gonna fall in love. Not me.

MRS. POTTS
Wait till you're a little older before you say that, Millie-
girl.

MILLIE
I'm old enough already. Madge can *stay* in this jerkwater
town and marry some ornery guy and raise a lot of dirty kids.
When I graduate from college I'm going to New York, and
write novels that'll shock people right out of their senses.

MRS. POTTS
You're a talented girl, Millie.

MILLIE
(*Victoriously*)
I'll be so great and famous—I'll never have to fall in love.

A BOY'S VOICE
(*From off stage, heckling* MILLIE)
Hey, Goongirl!

MILLIE
(*Spotting him in the distance*)
It's Poopdeck McCullough. He thinks he's so smart.

BOY'S VOICE

Hey Goongirl! Come kiss me. I wanna be sick.

MILLIE
(*Her anger roused*)
If he thinks he can get by with that, he's crazy.

(*She finds a stick with which to chastise her offender.*)

FLO

Millie! Millie! You're a grown girl now.

(MILLIE *thinks better of it, drops the stick and starts off.*)

MILLIE

See you this evening.

(*She goes off.*)

FLO
(*Wanting reassurance*)
Alan *will* be back, don't you think so, Helen?

MRS. POTTS

Of course he'll be back, Flo. He'll be back at Christmas time and take her to the dance at the Country Club, and they'll get married and live happily ever after.

FLO

I hope so.

(*Suddenly* MADGE *comes out the front door. She wears a hat and carries a small cardboard suitcase. There is a look of firm decision on her face. She walks straight to the gateway.*)

FLO
(*Stunned*)

Madge!

MADGE

I'm going to Tulsa, Mom.

MRS. POTTS
(*To herself*)

For heaven sake!

MADGE

Please don't get mad. I'm not doing it to be spiteful.

FLO
(*Holding her head*)

As I live and breathe!

MADGE

I know how you feel, but I don't know what else to do.

FLO
(*Anxiously*)

Now look, Madge, Alan's coming back Christmas. He'll take you to the dance at the Club. I'll make another new dress for you, and . . .

MADGE

I'm going, Mom.

FLO
(*Frantic*)

Madge! Listen to what I've got to say . . .

MADGE

My bus leaves in a few minutes.

FLO

He's no good. He'll never be able to support you. When
he does have a job, he'll spend all his money on booze. After
a while, there'll be other women.

MADGE

I've thought of all those things.

MRS. POTTS

You don't love someone cause he's perfect, Flo.

FLO

Oh, God!

BOYS' VOICES
(*In the distance*)
Hey, Madge! Hey, Beautiful! You're the one for me!

MRS. POTTS

Who are those boys?

MADGE

Some of the gang, in their hot-rod. (*Kisses* MRS. POTTS)
Good-bye, Mrs. Potts. I'll miss you almost as much as Mom.

FLO
(*Tugging at* MADGE, *trying to take the suitcase from
her*)
Madge, now listen to me. I can't let you . . .

MADGE

It's no use, Mom. I'm going. Don't worry. I've got ten dollars I was saving for a pair of pumps, and I saw ads in the Tulsa *World*. There's lots of jobs as waitresses. Tell Millie good-bye for me, Mom. Tell her I never meant it all those times I said I hated her.

FLO

(*Wailing*)

Madge . . . Madge . . .

MADGE

Tell her I've always been very proud to have such a smart sister.

(*She runs off now,* FLO *still tugging at her, then giving up and standing by the gatepost, watching* MADGE *in the distance.*)

FLO

Helen, could I stop her?

MRS. POTTS

Could anyone have stopped you, Flo?

(FLO *gives* MRS. POTTS *a look of realization.*)

BOYS' VOICES

Hey Madge!

You're the one for me!

FLO

(*Still watching* MADGE *in the distance*)

She's so young. There are so many things I meant to tell her, and never got around to it.

MRS. POTTS

Let her learn them for herself, Flo.

MRS. POTTS' MOTHER

Helen! Helen!

MRS. POTTS

Be patient, Mama.

(*Starts up the stairs to her back porch.* FLO *still stands in the gateway, watching in the distance.*)

CURTAIN